Transition beyond Denuclearisation

Chan Young Bang

Transition beyond Denuclearisation

A Bold Challenge for Kim Jong Un

palgrave
macmillan

Chan Young Bang
KIMEP University
Almaty, Kazakhstan

ISBN 978-981-15-4315-9 ISBN 978-981-15-4316-6 (eBook)
https://doi.org/10.1007/978-981-15-4316-6

This Palgrave Macmillan imprint is published by the registered company Springer Nature Singapore Pte Ltd.
The registered company address is: 152 Beach Road, #21-01/04 Gateway East, Singapore 189721, Singapore

I would like to dedicate this work to my wife, Youn Soo Kim, and son, Sung Won Bang, for their never-ending love and support of my work.

Preface

I am no outsider to the Korean conflict. I was born in 1936 in Ongjin, a city located on a small peninsula that extends just below the 38th parallel, so that when the Koreas were divided in 1945, my family lived in South Korean territory, even though we could only reach the mainland by boat.

On June 25, 1950, North Korean troops invaded and overran our province. My father ran a local hospital in the city, and we were thus unable to escape. For five months, until the joint South Korean and American forces expelled the North Korean army in January 1951, we lived under occupation.

All wars are bloody. As my father's hospital was converted into a field house for the North Korean soldiers, I personally witnessed death and other horrors of armed conflict. As a young boy, it terrified me. The Korean War is a particular tragedy because it was a violent clash between the same people—ideology divided family members and precipitated undue destruction and bloodshed.

Just before the North Korean troops retreated, they rounded up many from my province and hastily condemned them to death by firing squad. On that day, my grandfather, father, aunt and two uncles were captured, all of whom perished, save for my father. He narrowly escaped with his life after he was miraculously unstruck by the bullets. The survival of my father changed the course of my life, and he supported me throughout my educational pursuits and beyond.

This book is the synthesis of my ideas—a theory and a blueprint for North Korea to accept peaceful denuclearization and the rapid development of its economy for a chance at prosperity. I have monitored the situation in the Democratic People's Republic of Korea (DPRK) attentively over the years, and never once has a credible treatise, capturing the relevant nuances of the North Korean system and suggesting a viable blueprint for a way forward, been proposed.

My motivation to put forth a positive, amicable solution stems from an ardent desire to avert another devastating conflict and prevent others from the destruction that I experienced as a teenager. I fear that, if there were to be another escalation of armed conflict, it would far surpass the havoc and desolation wreaked by the Korean War in the 1950s. My conscience cannot bear the thought that I did not muster my full capabilities to attempt to contribute to a peaceful resolution.

At KIMEP University in Almaty, Kazakhstan, I established the DPRK Strategic Research Center and have recruited a team of prominent researchers who are dedicated to exploring peaceful prospects for a resolution to the North Korean nuclear crisis. I would like to acknowledge their input and contributions, which have been of the utmost value to me throughout the formulation of this book. I would also like to express my gratitude to the rest of the KIMEP University staff and faculty who accommodated me so that I could be most productive in my research while also leading the university.

I am also profoundly grateful to my family who give me their unwavering support, especially to my wife, Youn Soo Kim, and my three daughters, Elizabeth, Kima, and Jenny. My son, Sung Won Bang, provided moral support through our daily exercise together, which kept my mind fresh and sharp.

Notwithstanding the support of all of these individuals, all errors, shortcomings, and weaknesses that might be found in this text are exclusively my own responsibility.

Almaty, Kazakhstan Chan Young Bang

Contents

1 Introduction 1

1 Author's Qualifications and Rationale for the Book 1

2 Aim and Scope of the Research in This Book 4

2 Economic Decay and Failures of Reform in the DPRK 13

1 Introduction 13

2 Moving Beyond Traditional Analysis: Why Socialist Economies Fail and How the North Korean Case Deviates From the Paths of Other States 17

3 The Initial Distortion of Socialism in North Korea: Juche, *the* Suryong *System* 37

4 The Collapse of the Soviet Union and the Second Distortion of the System: Dysfunctional Marketization of the North Korean Economy 39

5 The Third Distortion of the System: The Detrimental Effects of International Sanctions and the Rise of the Donju 49

6 Conclusion 53

Bibliography 63

3 The Collapse Scenario: From Survival to Disintegration 67

1 Introduction 67

2 From Survival to Steady Erosion 68

3 The Endgame That Can Never Be Won 80

4 *The Necessity of "Carrots" and the Rationality of Kim Jong Un* 87
5 *Conclusion* 90
Bibliography 96

4 Economic Modernization Beyond Denuclearization 103
1 *Introduction* 103
2 *Necessary Conditions: Cost-Benefit Analysis and the Win-Win Scenario* 107
3 *Necessary Preconditions for North Korean Modernization: Transformation to Market Socialism and Integration with the World Economy* 112
4 *The North Korean Development Strategy: Strategic Approaches to Implementation of Market-Oriented Reform and Opening* 121
5 *Conclusion* 140
Bibliography 142

5 Conclusion 149
1 *The Possibility of North Korea's Survival with Weapons of Mass Destruction* 150
2 *Accepting Denuclearization to Maintain the Current Socioeconomic System* 152
3 *A Survival Strategy Through Rapid Economic Development* 153
4 *A Blueprint for "Transaction" and "Transformation" Led by the U.S.* 155

Index 159

About the Author

Chan Young Bang is the President of KIMEP University and Principal Investigator at the DPRK Strategic Research Center in Almaty, Kazakhstan. He was born and raised on the Ongjin Peninsula (present-day North Korea), before he fled to Seoul, South Korea at the onset of the Korean War. He taught economics for four years at the University of California, Los Angeles, and then obtained a tenured position as Professor of Economics at the University of San Francisco in 1978. At USF, he served as the Chairman of the Economics department for 16 years, and directed the university's Research Institute of Asian/Pacific Studies for over a decade.

In 1990, Dr. Bang was invited by Nursultan Nazarbayev, the President of Kazakhstan, to serve as his Economic Advisor and as the Vice Chairman of the Expert Committee, which the President himself chaired. In these roles, through the dissolution of the Soviet Union, he oversaw the introduction of market opening and privatization in Kazakhstan, leading to the nation's rapid development and emergence as the strongest economy in Central Asia.

He has been the recipient of numerous orders and awards, including for his contributions to education from the Kazakhstani Ministry of Education and Science, and the highest order that can be vested upon a foreigner who has made tangible contributions to the well-being of the Republic of Kazakhstan, the Dostyk Order. Dr. Bang has also been awarded many honorary degrees and professorships, among them an honorary doctoral degree from the Institute of Far-Eastern Studies of the Russian Academy of Sciences and distinguished professorships from

Beijing Normal University and Capital University of Economics and Business in China.

He has published numerous articles on prospects for peaceful settlement of the North Korean nuclear conflict, and this is his eighth book on the subject.

List of Figures

Fig. 3.1	Demonstrates the combined economic and sociopolitical effects that will destabilize and threaten the survival of the regime	86
Fig. 4.1	Represents the cost-benefit calculation that Kim Jong Un must conduct in his decision making	112

CHAPTER 1

Introduction

1 Author's Qualifications and Rationale for the Book

This book addresses the issue of North Korea's survival as a denuclearized, pacified and economically viable state, should the leader of the Democratic People's Republic of Korea (DPRK), Kim Jong Un, make the bold and audacious decision to abandon the current nuclear weapons program.

Built upon my analytical reasoning and intensive research over the past several decades, this book takes a genuine approach in the aspect that its main purpose is to put forth strategic solutions for the survival of the DPRK after denuclearization, while previous research on the DPRK has taken a one-sided approach, focusing too narrowly on how the application of threat could coerce the regime to denuclearize. I take a different approach.

In my research, "survival" means more than the mere continuation of the regime; it signifies dynamic, sustained economic development and prosperity through the drive for modernization. I have approached the task of writing this book driven by both personal and professional motivations, and I am fortunate in that both my personal background and my professional experience as an academic and a policy advisor to the first President of Kazakhstan, Nursultan Nazarbayev, have endowed me with what I consider to be a unique perspective on the North Korean conundrum.

C. Y. Bang, *Transition beyond Denuclearisation*,
https://doi.org/10.1007/978-981-15-4316-6_1

Born and raised on the Ongjin Peninsula, present-day North Korea, I was a teenager when the Korean War broke out in 1950, wreaking havoc upon my homeland and family. My father was a medical doctor who owned and operated a hospital; he devoted himself to treating the torrent of war victims who came flooding through his doors.

Before being evacuated together with part of my family in 1951, I personally witnessed the horrendous devastation of this fratricidal conflict, and I have lived with the knowledge that my close relatives toil under direct communist (that is, North Korean) rule. My family suffered several deaths by execution at the hands of the North Koreans. Upon my return to Ongjin after the end of armed conflict, I found my childhood home sequestered by the socialist party and my family members victim to utter desolation, having fallen seriously ill or otherwise executed by the state.

Naturally, the fact of being born in present-day North Korea does not automatically qualify me for the task of writing a book; this is why I rely on my own education and professional experience to assert throughout this book that I consider my vision for the future of North Korea as something unique, not found elsewhere in the literature about the DPRK.

I received my first three university degrees (a B.A. in History, 1954–1958, a second B.A. in Political Science, 1958–1960 and an M.A. in Economics, 1960–1964) at Yonsei University in Seoul. Later, I obtained an M.A. in Economics, 1968–1970 from University of Nevada, and finally a Ph.D. in Economics, 1977 at the University of Colorado.

During the late 1970s and the 1980s, I taught at UCLA and was fortunate enough to focus my research and lectures on economic transitions. I coupled this academic effort with more pragmatic endeavors, organizing numerous seminars and conferences that attracted the interest of economists and policymakers from both camps in the old war era. I served as Executive Director of the Research Institute of Asian/Pacific Studies at the University of San Francisco (1978–1988) then a Visiting Professor at the Institute of Economic Research at Hanyang University (1988–1989) before I became the Chief Economic Advisor to the first President of the Republic of Kazakhstan (1991–1993).

I received numerous invitations from the then Soviet Union during the late 1980s and early 1990s, as high-ranking members of the communist party wanted to gain insights into the strategic implications of security issues in Northeast Asia and, later, the dynamics of economic reform and transition.

Through my work, I met with numerous world leaders, such as former U.S. President George Bush Sr., U.K. Prime Minister Margaret Thatcher, Singapore's Prime Minister Lee Kuan Yew, U.S. Secretary of State James Baker, and the first Russian President, Boris Yeltsin. Of particular relevance to my work in this book is my direct experience with Mikhail Gorbachev, when he was still leading the Soviet Union, and my meetings with North Korean officials in China during the late 1990s. On both occasions, I came to the conclusion that blind attachment to the ideological, dogmatic principles of socialism was the main impediment to both Gorbachev and the North Korean elite to embracing a new set of ideas, a much-needed policy of radical reform and opening. Gorbachev wished to be remembered, in his own words to me, as a "dedicated communist" who refused to dismantle the socialist ideological implant.

As for the North Korean officials, I met with members of the inner circle during the rule of former leader Kim Jong Il and did my best to rely on an honest, if tough, account of reality: at that time, the DPRK was on its knees, crippled by the famine of the Arduous March, which claimed the lives of nearly a million people (according to most estimates). I was frank and honest in prescribing that the regime should initiate a series of crucial, market-oriented reforms accompanied by opening of the economy. This would require a paradigm change and removal of the mandate stemming from Kim Il Sung, transferring Kim Jong Il's source of legitimacy to the popular support of the people, garnered through rapid modernization. Additionally, I explained that, in order to override any destabilizing effects of opening, the regime would have to achieve spectacular, unprecedented growth, which would only be possible with the provision of a tremendous economic development fund.

The North Koreans did not receive my proposal well, and, in any case, the political milieu of that era was less than opportune for the negotiation of a multi-billion-dollar economic fund, to be provided by the international community. I was never again invited to consult with the DPRK, but today, twenty years later, I remain convinced that such a blueprint for rapid economic development and opening is the only way to ensure survival for North Korea and its people. This book carefully explains the details of my prescription for a contemporary implementation of economic modernization in the DPRK. Unlike his father, the situation in which Kim Jong Un now finds himself is advantageous for the introduction of market-oriented reform and opening. While the Supreme Leader's legitimacy traditionally stems from adherence to *Juche* ideology, the socialist system which Kim Jong Un inherited no longer bears the slightest resemblance to the principles on which it was founded decades ago. Thus, the burden of implementing *Juche* is relieved in such a way that allows for reform and opening to be initiated. Moreover, Kim Jong Un possesses a valuable bargaining chip that his father lacked—the nuclear weapons program. Now, the time is ripe for Kim Jong Un to approach the stakeholder nations with a plan for rapid, sustained economic development in return for denuclearization.

2 Aim and Scope of the Research in This Book

Over the last decades I have continuously worked toward one goal, seeking for the best possible answer to three fundamental questions, which will guide the research in this book from start to end:

1. "Can denuclearization be achieved peacefully, and if so, how?"
2. "Can North Korea survive beyond denuclearization, achieving peace and stability within the East Asia region, and if so, how?"
3. "Can the North Korean regime overcome the current external political pressure and its internal economic hardships, to dramatically modernize its economy beyond mere survival? If so, how?"

To my knowledge, no scholars in the field of North Korean studies have paid sufficient attention to these three essential questions, which represent the three-pronged scope of my work.

As the title implies (*Transition beyond denuclearization: political economy of modernization in the DPRK)*, this book deals with North Korean economic modernization from a political economist perspective and seeks to determine exactly which conditions must be fulfilled to ensure the survival of North Korea without nuclear weapons as an economically viable state. For the general public and more specialized readers alike, this book will identify a viable and credible blueprint for the DPRK to survive without nuclear weapons and become an economically prosperous country. Over the next three chapters, in the process of constructing this blueprint and developing the overarching theme of the book, I will address an array of sub-questions, which I list below, grouped by topic:

2.1 *The Contemporary North Korean Situation*

1. (A) Why is it widely perceived that nuclear weapons are an essential strategic asset for the survival of the Kim Jong Un regime?
   (B) Why did the North Korean nuclear weapons program develop?
   (C) Why is the DPRK's hostile foreign policy not the result of its nuclear weapons program but, on the contrary, the direct cause of the nuclear weapons program?
2. What conditions must be fulfilled for the DPRK to survive after relinquishing nuclear weapons?
3. What is the main cause of the prevailing distorted and dysfunctional social and economic systems in the DPRK?
4. How would regime change lead to acute instability and unfolding upheaval on the Korean peninsula?
5. While all socialist countries have either collapsed or transformed into market socialism without exception, how has the DPRK managed to survive?
6. Why can the DPRK no longer sustain the status quo that has enabled them to survive this long?
7. How does the DPRK's *Juche* ideology contradict economic modernization?

2.2 *Politics*

8. Even after all military and political threats are removed, why won't the DPRK be able to achieve growth and development?
9. Why has the United States' denuclearization policy objective, pursued over the past 30 years, singularly failed?
10. (A) Why can't the United States alone peacefully resolve denuclearization of the DPRK?
    (B) Why must the United States secure the unyielding commitment of the 5 stakeholders to enable the DPRK to survive and prosper economically?
11. (A) Why won't the "sticks" (economic sanction and other forms of pressure and threats) alone achieve the denuclearization of the DPRK? (B) What are the "carrots" (economic benefits and rewards) that will entice Kim Jon Un to accept denuclearization?
12. What credible evidence do we have about Kim Jong Un that will support his decision to exchanging nuclear weapons for economic modernization in a cost benefit analysis?

2.3 *Reform and Opening*

13. What are the preconditions that must be fulfilled before the DPRK can transform into market socialism?
14. Even with enormous compensation, why won't the DPRK be able to achieve economic modernization without reform and opening?
15. (A) What precisely does the DPRK's "Bright Future" mean?
    (B) How do Kim Jong Un's and President Trump's perceptions of the "Bright Future" for the DPRK differ?
16. How does Janos Kornai's definition for the reform of socialism fail to apply and properly expound on the prevailing economic and social situation in the DPRK?
17. Why must political reform precede economic reform in the DPRK?
18. Why is it impossible to achieve economic modernization without radical revision of the ruling *Juche* ideology?
19. (A) What can the DPRK learn from China and Vietnam (the two countries that have managed to successfully transform from socialism to market socialism)?
    (B) What are the DPRK's constrains in emulating China and Vietnam's experience in their political and economic transformations?
20. After reform and opening in the DPRK, why must GDP growth be 10% average per annum for a 10 year minimum in order to survive without nuclear weapons?
21. Why does the DPRK need a $300 billion development fund, at $30 billion per year, in order to survive with economic modernization and without nuclear weapons?
22. Why must South Korea be the largest contributor towards the DPRK's $300 billion development fund?

2.4 *Policy Prescription*

23. Can the DPRK survive and achieve optimum GDP growth without a well-conceived and viable development plan?
24. Will the provision of an economic development fund be sufficient without also making security guarantees?
25. How can isolated Special Economic Zones neutralize the acute instability that will emanate during reform and opening?

2.5 *Goals of the Research*

While answering each of these key questions throughout the following pages, the book aims to accomplish the following:

1. Provide a historical overview of the country's dynamic changes in the socialist system, having deviated from its past of conventional socialism, in view of exploring the reasons for gradual deterioration of the country's economy.
2. Describe the current situation in North Korea and invalidate the misconception that the malaises and distortions of the economy are caused by international sanctions, explaining that, rather, the dysfunctions of the system are inherent and only exacerbated by external pressure. In addition, I demonstrate the great inconsistencies and contradictions between reality and the ruling ideology.
3. Give a detailed description of prospects for the regime's survival through economic reform in a tangible sense (not merely cosmetic improvements), covering a range of preconditions (political and geopolitical barriers) and conditions (internal political reforms) with concentration on centralized and state-led "economic" modernization through legalization of business entities currently operating without legal sanction.
4. Put forth a strategic blueprint for the transformation of the dysfunctional North Korean economic and political systems into viable ones, achieving spectacular economic growth and modernization under the leadership of the ruling party, transforming North Korea into a viable and cooperative state in Northeast Asia.
5. Establish the necessity of an economic development fund, supported by all stakeholder nations and provided in exchange for North Korea's dismantlement of all nuclear weapons and other WMDs, with the understanding that this process does not aim to provoke regime change but rather to facilitate a transformation from totalitarianism to market socialism, adapted to the peculiarities of the North Korean system.
6. Outline the necessary conditions for implementation of the strategic blueprint for denuclearization, which will bring economic prosperity and permanent peace.

In essence, this book endeavors to demonstrate to all member nations of the Six-party Talks that the probability of the erosion of the foundations of the North Korean system are very high. The distorted state of the system, inherited by Kim Jong Un from his predecessors, will lead to the eventual collapse of the North Korean regime, an event which will have devastating and far-reaching consequences beyond the Korean Peninsula.

The consequential geopolitical disaster would result in destabilization of the region at large, affecting nearby allies Russia and China in addition to South Korean and Japan. This outcome, however, can be avoided if all of stakeholder nations cooperate and commit their unyielding support to the creation of a package deal—a blueprint for economic development in North Korea—which meets the interests of all members of the Six-party Talks. To prevent ultimate disaster, Kim Jong Un must be convinced by the collective stakeholders that economic development offers a far superior chance for regime survival than does the nuclear weapons program.

Existing literature on North Korea's economy lack macro analysis with close examination of historical circumstances, such as the constraints facing Chairman Kim which he inherited from his father and grandfather before him. Similarly, previous research hasn't taken into due account that reform of the system will require that political hurdles are removed, preceded by a paradigm change that will define the fundamental attributes of the economic development strategy. In dealings with North Korean politics, past scholarly work has focused heavily on the nuclear issue and geopolitics, thus ignoring the question of how the regime can develop its economy after denuclearization. To this day, no coherent, viable policy proposal, demanding the participation of all of the stakeholder nation, has been put forth.

In short, past research has failed to produce a coherent solution to North Korea's predicament because it has failed to pose the correct question. Rather than asking "How do we force North Korea to abandon the nuclear weapons program?" one ought to be asking "How long can North Korea survive without viable economic reform?" Continuing this thought, what would be the consequences if the regime failed? What must the stakeholder nations do to avoid collapse?

By posing the latter question, this book is designed to surpass the limitations of existing North Korean studies and expand the discourse into future-oriented studies for change in the communist country. Composed of three parts that see North Korea within the framework of its past, present and future, each chapter puts forth a main question.

For future-oriented North Korean studies, the book deals with why the five-party involved countries have so far tried but failed to denuclearize the North. It examines the scenarios in which North Korea could opt for a future that all five parties involved are satisfied with. There are two main ways that North Korea can seek regime survival: (1) safeguard its legitimacy while possessing nuclear weapons; and (2) give up nuclear weapons and seek survival through a guarantee of security and economic funds. Through a cost-benefit analysis, the book sought to find the most rational option for the survival of the North's regime and a deal that all five parties involved could embrace. Through this cost-benefit calculation, it emphasizes that for Kim Jong Un that the only option for survival is through abandoning nuclear weapons and securing legitimacy through the improvement of economic welfare. He still has the opportunity to make a wise choice, but there is not much time.

First, this work asks: How and why did the DPRK brand of socialism fail? The opening of the book inquires as to whether reform could have prevented the series of disasters in the 1990s, most notably the Arduous March. Then, it asks what the implications for the contemporary DPRK may be. It begins by tracing the main characteristics of North Korea's economic development since the era of Kim Il Sung and the gradual distortions of the socioeconomic system under the rule of Kim Jong Il and, finally, under Kim Jong Un.

The main argument here is that North Korea, which started off as a socialist economy, has deviated from traditional socialism over time and developed its own unique socioeconomic system, characterized by features of military totalitarianism and hereditary succession of power grafted onto an extractive economic system. Over the decades, three major series of distortions contributed to modifying the nature of the North Korean system from socialism to a uniquely dysfunctional economy.

These three distortions can be made to overlap with the three Kims: the era of Kim Il Sung, in which *Juche* ideology and dynastic power were created and implemented; the era of Kim Jong Il, in which the country faced the consequences of the disintegration of the Soviet Union and heavy militarization; and, finally, the era of Kim Jong Un, in which the country now risks total collapse under the weight of international sanctions and bottom-up marketization, and in which power is administered by the leader within a small coalition system.

The traditional analytic lens (Kornai), which proposed to explain the transition from socialist systems to either a full-fledged capitalism or a mixed system (market socialism), is analyzed, revealing limitations when applied to the case of North Korea. The notion of market socialism, in turn, also presents constraints, although it has been successfully used to analyze the Chinese and Vietnamese cases, leading to speculation that it may be used for the DPRK as well. The DPRK case is established as differing from all previous instances of either traditional socialism or transitional economies, and it has to be analyzed in the light of unique ideology and unique historical contingency (the division of the peninsula).

Next, I ask on what grounds it can be argued that the current Kim Jong Un regime is most likely in the process of collapse and would be even in the case of sanctions and pressure relief. Having explored how the North Korean regime evolved under the leadership of Kim Jong Un this segment of the book explains the pillars of its current viability and whether the system can be sustained in the future—if yes, for how long? If not, what might the consequences be?

The regime rests on five pillars that, in contemporary time, are crumbling under the weight of economic sanctions, lack of resources and funds and the erosion of the ideology due to external information. By examining the extent to which these foundations are being corroded, I reach the conclusion that the collapse of the North Korean regime is imminent and its signs are definite. Assuming that Chairman Kim is also cognizant of this reality, I posit that he is now faced with the choice between retaining or abandoning the nuclear weapons program which has served very well so far as an instrument of domestic legitimacy, an international bargaining chip and justification for enormous socioeconomic sacrifices on the part of the people. To conclude this argument, both cost and benefits of each choice are laid out, though they are considered only in part, to be fully explained in the remainder of the book.

The final segment of the book asks, in the event that Kim Jong Un chooses denuclearization, what viable options are available and which preconditions must be in place to ensure that the benefits of this decision outweigh the costs? What is the most effective modernization path the DPRK could take beyond denuclearization and mere survival, assuming that Kim Jong Un's rational calculation of cost vs. benefit will lead him to opt for reform and opening?

I postulate that the overall benefits of denuclearization outweigh the costs. Many experts have been skeptical about Chairman Kim's decision to denuclearize since 2017, arguing that the regime will still survive even if they ultimately do not embrace denuclearization. I disagree on the grounds that Kim Jong Un seems to be a rational and capable leader who is unlikely to opt for such a costly option.

Rapid economic modernization without nuclear weapons is the only path to regime survival. However, the country does not yet possesses the vision, funds and institutions necessary to create a roadmap out of its current impasse. Thus, ultimately I put forward a concrete blueprint, or strategic plan, for rapid market-oriented reform and opening, along with the preconditions necessary to its implementation. In the blueprint, I stress that not only the DPRK but all stakeholders must participate in helping the country out of its present deadlock and normalize it as a trade and negotiation partner in the international market, resolving decades-old conflict in the region and bringing a prosperous future for all.

CHAPTER 2

Economic Decay and Failures of Reform in the DPRK

1 Introduction

Chapter 2 seeks to move beyond conventional economic thought on the nature of the North Korean economy. Before the trajectory of the economic and political systems of the DPRK can be explored, however, I must examine the factors that have altered the centralized planned economy into one so dysfunctional that it will never achieve sustained development and modernization without a radical paradigm shift, founded on market-oriented reform and opening.

When Kim Jong Un came to power in 2011, he inherited not only the Supreme Leadership but also an economic system that has grown severely dysfunctional and distorted from its original form of a socialist economy. In spite of this, the North Korean regime under Kim Jong Un has not yet met the demise of other socialist states, although no radical economic reform has been enacted and the nuclear weapons program remains intact.

Why is this so? In this chapter I make an important distinction between outright privatization and the regime's attempts at introducing cosmetic improvement measures, as well as a system of benign oversight which involves the deliberate acquiescence of state-owned enterprises for unofficial use—effectively "rented out" for private business activity. Consequential to this is the necessity to distinguish between reforms and improvements; that is, between radical changes that fundamentally alter the nature of any given system and smaller, *ad hoc* modifications that seek to improve the functionality of a system without essentially modifying its

C. Y. Bang, *Transition beyond Denuclearisation*,
https://doi.org/10.1007/978-981-15-4316-6_2

nature. Therefore, the chapter explains the conceptual nuances and their application to the specific case of North Korea—of "reform within the system", "change", "improvement" as they have been, at times, too loosely applied to the study of North Korea's evolution over the last two decades. Finally, to fully understand the case of North Korea one ought to define what the contemporary North Korean economy looks like and whether it resembles any socialist state to which it is often compared.

Thus, the purpose of the chapter is to:

1. Establish an understanding of the unique quagmire that is the contemporary North Korean economy, being entirely unconventional and riddled with distortion and illegality in its historical context;
2. Explain how and why the North Korean economy suffered a gradual, steady decline over the past five decades but it did not follow the demise of other former socialist economies;
3. Demonstrate the system's lack of resemblance to any normal socialist economy and explain their refusal to embrace market-oriented reform and opening;
4. Explain how and why the North Korean government failed to implement any of the meaningful reforms that have transformed other former socialist economies into full-fledged market economies.

My hypothesis, supported by recent accounts of the North Korean leader,[1] is that despite past failures to enact meaningful reform, Kim Jong Un's most ardent aspiration is to leave behind a legacy as the Supreme Leader who oversaw the transformation of the DPRK into a politically viable and economically prosperous state. This feat, however, is fundamentally impossible at present, due to the deformed nature of the economic system, and it would remain so even if the pressure of military confrontation with the US and internationally-imposed sanctions were to be withdrawn simultaneously.

Turning to the reasons for the incurably dysfunctional nature of the North Korean system, in this chapter I will analyze three main factors: division between north and south, disintegration of the Soviet Union, and sanctions

1.1 *The Division and Rivalry Between the North and the South*

The fact that North and South Korea were born in opposition to each other is the defining feature of every political and economic choice that Pyongyang has made over the decades. It is not possible to fully grasp the nuances of the North Korean state's behavior without fully understanding this. Since 1948, North Korea has competed with the South for the same territorial and ethnic entity engaging in the ideological demolition of "the other" as its own political legitimacy is predicated on the illegitimacy of the opponent.

This rivalry has remained unchanged for nearly 70 years in both quantitative and qualitative aspects.

In quantitative terms, North Korea has initially published statistics on its economic growth, attempting to show a dynamic growth, with claims of two-digit GDP expansion rates during the 1960s. Relevant studies[2] have demonstrated that such statistics were largely inflated and unreliable. North Korea has ceased any statistical publication related to macro and micro economic matters since the late 1960s. The quantitative competition between the two Koreas however was not only measured and compared over GDP, but also in relation to per capita income, the number of square miles of pavement, or even embassies hosted abroad. Ultimately, with a value of $1.6 trillion, South Korea's economy today is 50 times larger than the North's $32 billion, while the South's per capita income is estimated to be 25 to 30 times higher,[3] indicating that South Korea is clearly victorious in the rivalry of quantity.

In qualitative terms, since 1948 and until the 1990s, North Korea repeatedly claimed that it provided a superior socioeconomic model whereby citizens were provided with lifetime employment and rewarded with an extensive welfare network for education, healthcare, and housing. Perhaps even more important is the strong narrative in North Korean propaganda that the South was a destitute country, nearly a colony of the US, where slavery, alienation, human rights violations and immense social inequality were the norm. The DPRK has recently relinquished this narrative as the population is becoming increasingly aware of the economic divide and the level of prosperity in the South.

Since the era of Kim Il Sung, the competition between North and South, Socialism vs. Capitalism, has been cemented as a fundamental attribute of the North's doctrine. Should this rivalry ever waiver, the entire ideological control system would break down. Therefore, reinforcement of ideological indoctrination and claims to legitimacy through enormous military spending has become essential to the survival of the regime, while any incentives to secure the state of the economy are purely ideological.

1.2 The Collapse of the Soviet Union and the Failure of Socialist Economy

Until 1991, the DPRK functioned as a normal socialist state with a functioning centrally-planned economy. After the disintegration of the USSR, however, North Korea was left without access to what had historically been their primary external market. This was a heavy blow to trade which also decreased North Korea's import of capital goods. Following the collapse of the socialist system in the Soviet Union and other communist nations in the Eastern Bloc, the state decided to import commodities instead of capital goods to promote macroeconomic stability in its economy. Such restrictions on the import of capital goods effectively accelerated the collapse of North Korea's manufacturing sector, among other devastating effects.

1.3 Aggravation from Sanctions during the 2010s

Since the escalation of internationally-imposed economic sanctions, the North Korean economy has entered a new era of system distortion. This growing burden, which began following initial missile tests in 2006 but have particularly expanded in scope since Kim Jong Un's rise to power in 2012, has pushed the regime to the brink of losing all control of the official economy. As unauthorized markets and moneylenders build power through trade, industrial and agricultural production plummets, and bureaucratic systems intensify in exploitation and terror, marketization[4] will not suffice to rectify the severe distortions of the North Korean economy. Because the nature of the system itself is deeply at odds with the characteristics of other socialist and communist economies, any steps the regime may take to improve individual facets of an inherently dysfunctional and inefficient economy without altering its fundamental nature are destined to fail—or provoke social and humanitarian calamity. Economic decline has turned North Korea into an international pariah entangled in aid dependency, and it has forced the government to passively accommodate growing unofficial bottom-up marketization among half-hearted attempts at top-down reforms within the system. The failure of reforms in the DPRK has only been partially examined so far, usually without a proper analysis of *the nature* of these reforms. There is also little distinction in the conventional literature between the type of changes that the North Korean leadership can attempt to enable within the limits of the paradigm of the official ideology (*Juche*) and those that alter the nature of the system itself.

The analysis in the chapter loosely follows the historical trajectory of North Korean economy and its downfall. The chapter collocates in time significant economic measures that the conventional literature periodically interprets either as symptoms of transformation, or stages of a prolonged permutation. However, I believe that while there are some differences between the eras of Kim Il Sung (1948–1994), Kim Jong Il (1994–2011) and Kim Jong Un era (2012–present) in my view these are not indicative of any substantive change in the style of governance that underpinned the North Korean variety of socialism and its distortions. Therefore, while most scholarly work follow this periodization, I divide the analysis of North Korean economy along three phases, *each representing a further distortion of the original socialist system in North Korea*. These are the Cold War period, when North Korea's economy first grew and then plateaued (1953–1989); the crisis period, triggered by the disintegration of the Soviet Union and socialist economies worldwide, when North Korea attempted to modify individual sectors of its economy (1990–2011); finally, the last stage, characterized by the growing burden of international sanctions and the rise of a new elite that stems from the North Korean nuclear weapons program (2012–2019).

2 Moving Beyond Traditional Analysis: Why Socialist Economies Fail and How the North Korean Case Deviates From the Paths of Other States

The failures of the DPRK is not an isolated case: all socialist economies experienced the same kinds of challenges. Every socialist economic system suffered from poor and unreliable statistical output, relied on closed-door trading within the Eastern Bloc, and were classified as delinquent loan recipients by international financial institutions. Thus, any attempts to improve the economic condition singularly failed, falling short of raising the standard of living and the GDP.[5]

What are the compelling reasons that all socialist states, including North Korea, are unable to achieve sustained economic growth on par with that realized by capitalist, market economies such as China, Vietnam, or Kazakhstan? In other words, why is it that all socialist states are, without exception, stagnated and deprived from economic prosperity, and how can we apply this concept to the North Korean case?

2.1 *Why Socialist Economies Fail*

Economic failure cannot be properly analyzed as a matter of poor performance; it must be explained through a coherent understanding of the political nature of the system that dictates the economy, and compatibility between the nature of the socialist state and the nature of economic reforms. A number of fundamental characteristics determine the structure of the socialist planned economic system and its inherent inability to achieve high, sustained economic growth.

First, the challenges and difficulties facing the socialist system come from the fundamental difference between capitalist and socialist systems—ownership structure. In a capitalist economy, the vitality of economic activity stems from dynamic elements that are, at the most basic level, rooted in greed. Competition, innovation, efficiency and the motivation to build enterprises that last are all underpinned by the desire to possess material wealth and intangible assets, such as fame. All of these dynamic elements are made possible by the right to individual ownership. In a socialist economy, on the other hand, all means of production are in the hands of the state, and the underlying principle is the ideal of collectivism, in which each individual contributes for the good of all.[6] This lack of individual ownership deprives the economy of the vitalizing, dynamic factors necessary for viable economic growth, and it is the principal weakness of a socialist economic system.

Second, the socialist system faces numerous difficulties in the collection and preparation of relevant information and materials for the centrally planned economy. Even if the central planning authorities overcome the problems of information collecting and material compensation and motivation, they are unable to collect information to coordinate all necessary economic activities, such as production, distribution and capital accumulation. Furthermore, even assuming that the central planning authorities are able to collect relevant information and statistics needed for efficient resource allocation, they will never be able to draw up a coherent, central plan without committing errors because the information and data are too vast.

Third, most relevant information needed by socialist economic planners to formulate rational and objective plans exists in a fluid and unfinished form. Therefore, they face difficulties in collecting and converting data into a coherent economic plan. Furthermore, as economic conditions change continually, data and information collected yesterday is no longer valid or applicable to tomorrow.

Fourth, the socialist planned economic system is inherently conducive to totalitarian leadership systems. Therefore, the central planning authority, which governs the coordination of economic activities, can not only monopolize all the powers concerning the allocation of resources but also control every aspect of human life (such as jobs and compensation).

2.2 The Problems of "state ownership of means of production" and "the law of value"

The absence of the "law of value" and the "distortion of resource allocation" in the socialist system are the key factors that make rational economic calculations impossible.[7] Prices of goods determined by the "interaction of supply and demand" in a competitive market are key to efficient resource allocation and economic activity. However, under the socialist planned economic system, in which all means of production are owned by the state, no law of value, such as a market economic system, can exist. According to L. Von Mises, in modern complex economies, private ownership of the means of production is a prerequisite for rational economic calculation.[8] His key argument is that, without "personal ownership of the means of production," the market cannot exist. The reason for this is that, even if the means of production are changed from one state enterprise to another, supply and demand are monopolized solely by the state agency, therefore, the state exercises its ownership and there is only one seller, thus failing to establishment a market.

Naturally, a monetary price cannot be objectively established unless the market exists. Without the currency price reflecting the "relative scarcities" of the various means of production, rational economic calculation is impossible.

The absence of a "law of value" under the socialist economic system and the resulting distortion of resource allocation are insurmountable obstacles that are faced not only by North Korea's socialist system, but a universal phenomenon that appears in all socialist countries. Joseph Stalin and Kim Il Sung both conceded that the inability to objectively establish the "law of value" had a certain negative impact, but, nevertheless, this could not exert an insurmountably destructive effect on the socialist production process.

However, both Kim Il Sung and Stalin overlooked the inability to objectively calculate the price of production based on the labor and material input if all "supply" goes according to plan, making a coherent calculation impossible. The law of value can only prevail in a market system. In a competitive market economy, prices are determined as a result of the exchange of goods and services and the interaction of supply and demand by many independent sellers and buyers. In a socialist system, there is no market as there is only one seller. North Korea's economic system, in which almost all means of production are under state enterprise, thus under state ownership, lacks a market and, therefore, the "law of value" cannot prevail.

2.3 *The Problems of a Centralized Planned Economy*

The fundamental defect of a socialist centrally planned system lies in the fact that rational coordination by any central authority is practically impossible because information and knowledge of all economic activities in the society are incomplete and unfixed.

Under the complex modern market economy system, hundreds of thousands of producers decide on what is considered the most economically feasible of the numerous product variants based on the relative information and experiences. The responsibility for coordination falls on individual companies. Can many of these decisions be completely replaced by central planning authorities? Can many of these decisions be made simultaneously and collectively by the central planning authorities? In other words, planning authorities must make decisions on billions of variables and equations simultaneously, including labor output, wages, costs, prices, projected returns and profits on investment, materials, raw materials and goods needed for production. Some scholars estimated that this task would take 30,000 years, even if modern high-tech electronic calculators were used by central authorities to fully balance, carefully examine and condense all decisions into a single economic plan.[9]

The key issue with regard to economic planning is not that the number of variables and sets to be determined by the planning authorities is immense, but that they exist in a state of flux, unfixed and in a state of constant change. This means that those in charge of economic planning are unable to collect reliable information needed for a reasonable economic plan. Even if they can get all the information they need, the "decision" in the absence of "market prices" that reflect the relative value of economic goods is devoid of economic meaning. Hayek points out that the knowledge needed for the coordination of all economic activities in society is fluid, and the knowledge owned by one individual is very partial and only incomplete.[10] Ludwig Von Mises recognized the market as a dynamic process of human value and interaction. This means that economic calculation requires a clear understanding of the nature of the exchange relationship established by market prices.[11] Under the socialist system, the "state ownership" of the means of production and the central plan deprives the function and role of market prices essential to rational economic calculation.

2.4 *The Centralized Planned Economic System and Left-leaning Totalitarianism*

The "state ownership" under the socialist system controls and suppresses everything, not only the freedom of choice granted to man, but also the desires and hopes. As Hayek stated, a leader under a socialist planned economy controls and suppresses every facet of human life by controlling all economic activities.[12] This means that people's daily choices (i.e. where they work, what kind of food they should eat and at which restaurant, when to change their shoes, how to think, etc.) are all controlled and regulated by their rulers.[13]

2.5 *What Sets the Failure of the North Korean System Apart from all Other Socialist Failures*

Conventional practice outlines the fundamental differences between capitalist and socialist economies, but the North Korean case is unique in that it doesn't fit the normal pattern. Two relevant issues have historically set the DPRK apart from its former socialist allies.

First, North Korea has long outlived the Soviet Union and the Eastern Bloc. The question here then, is: "how did North Korea survive?"

Second, North Korea has not implemented any of the reforms of the system that have transformed countries like Kazakhstan, China and Vietnam into either full-fledged market or market socialist economies.[14] The question here is: "what path did North Korea follow after the demise of the Soviet Union?"

In other words, given the two main economic systems of modern history—socialism and capitalism—and the possibility of a hybrid system such as market socialism, North Korea presents a unique conundrum because of the following idiosyncrasies:

- It differs from traditional socialist economies.
- It has not conducted market-oriented reforms (through transition to either a full-fledged market or market socialist system), in the way that China or Vietnam have.

To explain all these peculiarities, I proceed as follows:

1. I first illustrate the characteristics that North Korean and other socialist economies have in common and those which differ.
2. Then, I explain why the analytic frameworks commonly used to describe the transformation of socialist economies with market-oriented reforms and capitalism is not adequate for the case of the DPRK.
3. Then, I illustrate the case of market socialism, and explain why the DPRK has not yet adopted it.
4. Finally, I explain how one can truly make sense of the North Korean case.

2.6 The Limits of Traditional Analytical Framework: Kornai and the Political Economy of Socialism

One cannot provide a coherent explanation of how the North Korean economy became so dysfunctional and distorted from its socialist roots without addressing the political nature of the state, which dictates the paradigm of economic development. To address the situation in North Korea, one should first assess the common traits of all communist regimes. As I mentioned, one of the features of most of the conventional literature on the North Korean economy is that, in assessing the DPRK's poor economic record, it assumes both the ability and the lack of political will of the government to adopt radical economic reform; therefore, economic failure is largely attributed to incompetence, mismanagement, or external factors. This assumption has never been tested, and this is where a number of shortcomings in analysis arise.

The traditional studies of economic transition, particularly Kornai, are useful insofar as they explain the general traits of traditional socialism and how a socialist system can be characterized as undertaking transformation.[15] To this end, Kornai proposes that we look at five core components which constitute the socialist system—the communist party armed with socialist ideology, nationalization of all means of production, central planning, bureaucratic controlling mechanisms, and totalitarianism—with the understanding that by observing change in at least two of these, one could assume that the system is undergoing reform.

The issue with this framework is not that the question that it poses is wrong but that it differs from the approach necessary to analyze the North Korean system. Rather than asking "What constitutes reform of the system?" we ought to, instead, ask "How can a socialist economy transform into a more efficient and productive system, enabling them to ultimately achieve sustained economic development?" To answer this question, we must consider a sixth core component of the DPRK system—marketization from below.

The component overlooked by Kornai and others is, therefore, the issue of a traditional market, defined by the activities of many independent sellers and buyers with the means of producing and bringing goods to the market, having determined the price of goods through the interaction of supply and demand. In the contemporary North Korean economy, more than 50% of the national GDP is generated in the unofficial market by private sellers and producers who "lease" means of production and human resources from the state through a process of acquiescence, also dubbed "benign oversight". These unauthorized market activities thrive in a number of North Korean industries: from tourism and entertainment to construction. Without consideration of this crucial sixth element, marketization from below, Kornai's framework cannot accurately explain the prevailing condition of the North Korean system.

Having established the necessity of marketization[16] to the transformation of the socialist economy into an efficient system, capable of precipitating high, sustained economic development, let's demonstrate how the traditional framework reveals limitations when applied to the North Korean case. It is true that North Korea started off as a socialist system, and therefore shares essential components of socialism, all of which contribute to the system's inability to reform without a profound change of nature—the cosmetic improvement measures which have been introduced cannot qualify as concrete change nor do they signal any true alterations of the system.

The North Korean system has, however, grown severely distorted over time through the introduction of markets and other improvement measures to the original socialist, extractive totalitarian system. To comprehend the extent of this distortion in transforming the system, we must analyze the five components proposed by Kornai, keeping in mind the sixth component of marketization, to position the North Korean case alongside them. By doing so, we can verify that although more than two out of five of the framework's essential components have undergone transition, the system cannot be classified as either a market economy or a market socialist system.

The five essential components constituting the socialist systems can be summarized as follows:

1. The Communist Party: a dictatorship is established based on political ideology centered on the notions of class struggle and aimed at the establishment of a proletarian dictatorship. This reality is all-encompassing, across the spectrum of political, social and economic affairs. The prime historical example of such a system in action is the Soviet Union, where the socialist economy system was born. With the success of their revolution in 1917, Lenin and his followers, imbued with the ideology of communism, gained power. During the next two years, from 1917 to 1918, the newly established communist regime nationalized all major means of production, from banks, heavy industries, transportation, communication and foreign trade, and then established and carried out the first Five Year Plan from 1928 to 1933.
2. Nationalization: within the socialist reality, as already pointed out by Hayek and Von Mises, the system can only work by preventing any private ownership of the means of production. In all socialist states, it is not the state ownership of the means of production that results in an official ruling ideology; rather it is the official ruling ideology that leads to the state owning all means of production. Marx and Engels were convinced that, in order to end exploitation by the capitalist class and unequal income distribution, all means of production have to be confiscated from the capitalist class and transferred to the possession of the state
3. Central planning: once all the means of production have been nationalized, the centralized planned economy takes the place of pre-existing economic structures. Once the nationalization of all major production means is complete, the authorities in power establish and carry out a centralized economy plan. As a result, private corporations and autonomous actors vanish from the market, and all competition between these actors ceases. All information and decision processes regarding production and distribution are monopo-

lized by the centralized planning authorities. The horizontal relationship once existing between actors in the economy is now replaced by a vertical relationship where orders are issued and obeyed. As Kornai pointed out, once the political structure, official ideology, nationalization and dominant role of the state have been established, the mechanisms of bureaucratic control come into action.[17] With the state controlling all production means, producing and distributing goods according to its plan, the state becomes able to exercise the authority to regulate and control the everyday lives and activities of its people. Everything is controlled and regulated by the party—everything, including where people are to live, what jobs they should work at, and how much food and basic goods they are to be supplied with.

4. Bureaucratic control mechanisms: the socialist system devises mechanisms of bureaucratic control (ideological indoctrination, rationing system, punishment). With the party controlling all power, any groups or individuals that challenge or deviate from the basic tenets of the party, i.e. the ideologies of socialism, are suppressed and persecuted without mercy. The distribution system serves as a material means of control and is at the core of the bureaucratic controlling mechanism, preventing people from leaving their assigned workplace and residence, thus serving as a means of limiting the freedom of movement. Differentiating the quantity and quality of distributed goods according to the degree of loyalty shown by individuals allows the state to instill higher levels of loyalty and induce the arduous zeal of patriotism among the people. In addition to careful control through economic bureaucratic controlling measures, the party also employs physical controlling measures such as the imprisonment and execution of dissenting individuals. Once the Communist Party dominates all power it realizes the teachings of Communist ideologies by nationalizing major production means and carrying out a centralized economy plan, while putting bureaucratic controlling measures into action. As Hayek originally stated, a ruler that controls and coordinates all economic activities not only controls those aspects that humans consider important when leading their lives, but everything down to those aspects that humans consider to be trivial.
5. Totalitarianism: the socialist system mutates into totalitarianism with absolute control over the lives, education, movement and even

the thought of its citizens. This is carried out through the building of an extensive apparatus of repression, signifying a state of absolute control in which all means of production are dominated by the ruler, who is thus able to decide and control every aspect of people's lives, from what basic human goals should be satisfied to what people should believe and strive for. This means control over not only the external conditions of human lives, but absolute control that extends down to the internal values and personal beliefs of the people. What many people misunderstand is that the establishment of a planned economy had the accidental and unpredictable result of militarizing social structures. But as has been pointed out by D. Lavoie, it was not the establishment of a planned economy that inadvertently led to militarization; establishing a planned economy, in itself, means to militarize. Once the Communist Party exercises absolute power and, according to its dominant ideology, nationalizes production means and puts a bureaucratic controlling mechanism into action, this completes left wing totalitarianism.

2.7 *What has Happened in the DPRK if Not Reform?*

At this point, if one wanted to test that which Kornai, D. Lavoise, Smith proposes, the key question would be: *Have at least two of these five components undergone change in North Korea*? The answer is "yes, more than two, to a degree". Yet, in spite of this, the regime has not changed the fundamental nature of the system. No top-down reform has actually taken place in the DPRK (reforms which could be defined as "reform of the system" if we were to apply Kornai's framework.).

The fundamental question then is: "If no meaningful reform of the system has taken place, then what has happened in the DPRK?" The short, preliminary answer is that the 1990s economic crisis and the famine brought a number of unspoken concessions and modifications within the system (but not of the system itself) that the government has reluctantly tolerated, enabling private individuals to participate in unofficial market activities, in order to alleviate social discontent.[18] This happened because even in North Korea a certain level of social contract does exist, if not between the state and the citizens, certainly between the government and selected economic agencies, as well as among a handful of individuals and small groups.

However, this short answer is not sufficient to fully account for the combination of three unique factors in the North Korean case. These factors are:

1. the survival of North Korea after the demise of the Soviet Union and the fall of the communist Eastern Bloc;
2. the fact that despite its survival, North Korea has not altered any core elements of its system in a way that could be classified as transformation; and
3. the fact that in spite of all of the above, the state has muddled through for 25 years since the breakout of the famine in 1995.

First, it must be acknowledged that Kornai's framework has drawbacks that prevent it from accurately analyzing the North Korean case. I will address this by explaining how many elements have been modified and then exploring why their modification did not constitute market-oriented reform. Then, I will explore an alternative framework—loosely denominated "market socialism"—that in the recent decade has been adopted by a number of scholars, to try to account for North Korean uniqueness; however, even this latest research fails to capture the essence of North Korea uniqueness, and, thus, I will turn to why.

In the following Table 2.1, I demonstrate, according to the framework originally proposed by Kornai, what a socialist country that has actually embraced market-oriented reform looks like and compare this with what has happened in North Korea since the 1990s crisis[19]:

As outlined above, not only two but four essential components of socialism originally proposed by Kornai have undergone substantial change, to varying degrees, in North Korea since the fall of the Soviet Union. In spite of all this, no one can argue that viable reform has fundamentally transformed the system into one of market socialism or otherwise altered the extractive totalitarian system. It appears then, that the North Korean case presents special circumstances—historically and currently active in its politics, society and economy—that lie beyond the analytic limits of traditional framework put forth by Kornai.

Once again, one has to observe that the limits of Kornai's analysis are due to the fact that, when he analyzed the decadence and demise of the Eastern Bloc and the Soviet Union, he was primarily looking at a traditional type of socialist economy. This type is defined by collective ownership of the means of production by the state, and is one in which the

Table 2.1 Outlines the differences between the transformation of a totalitarian socialist system according to Kornai and the changes within the system that have taken place in North Korea

What transformation of a totalitarian socialist system should look like according to Kornai's framework	*What has happened in North Korea since the 1990s socioeconomic crisis*
Removal of the Communist Party's dictatorship, characterizing traditional socialism, which is based on political ideology of class struggle and the proletariat dictatorship with a socialist revolution.	This has partially happened in the DPRK, as the references to communism have been abandoned in the constitution since 2008 while the *Juche* ideology, which was grafted onto traditional socialism, has suffered a decline and no longer enjoys popular support[a].
Preventing the state from interfering with private ownership of the means of production, therefore freeing economic activities.	This has also happened, to a degree, as the government allowed the use of state-owned means of production for private use by benign oversight, thus allowing marketization from below, beginning in the 1990s[b].
Removal of any constraints that historically result from a centralized planned economy.	This has also partially happened because of the disintegration of the state manufacturing sector; although the government claims to plan each step of the national economy, the reality is that private markets account for over 50% of the national GDP.
Removal of the system of bureaucratic control, namely ideological indoctrination, the rationing system, the public distribution of goods and services, and punishment for political, social or economic activities that are arbitrarily considered to be subversive.	This is also partially happened, as North Korean authorities can no longer maintain the rationing system to distribute food and services to its citizens, due to a large extent to the disintegration of the state manufacturing sector and the waning of ideological indoctrination, thus eroding the socialist system.

[a]Tudor, Daniel & Pearson, James. 2015. *North Korea Confidential*. Clarendon: Tuttle Publishing. p. 22

[b]Lankov, Andrei. 2013. *The Real North Korea: Life and Politics in the Failed Stalinist Utopia*. Oxford: Oxford University Press. p. 131; Smith, Hazel. 2015. *North Korea: Markets and Military Rule*. Cambridge: Cambridge University Press; Fifield, Anna. 2019. *The Great Successor: The Secret Rise and Rule of Kim Jong Un*. New York: John Murray

transition from socialism to capitalism rests on the assumption that the state is willing to relinquish collective ownership and rights to use in favor of individual ownership with full property rights. He did not consider the resourceful accommodations the North Korean system has made to acquiesce the means of production for private use, which has precipitated the process of unofficial marketization from below.

As I will explain in the next three sections, the North Korean system has progressively deviated from the socialist norm over the decades. Here, it is important to make one relevant point: the collapse of the Soviet Union and the Eastern Bloc came with an open admission of ideological, as well as economic, failure: authorities admitted that socialism had singularly failed. In consequence, the adoption of capitalism and market relations became inevitable.

This has never happened in North Korea. The DPRK constitution, in each and every edition and revision, preserves a fundamental article stating that the state pursues a socialist struggle in a system in which the state owns the means of production. In this context, it makes little sense to discuss presumed "change" or "reform of the system" for North Korea, but rather, it is better to hypothesize a resourceful adoption that does not change the fundamental nature of the system but seeks to cure some of its inefficiencies without implementing radical market-oriented reform.

2.8 *An Alternative Hypothesis: Market Socialism in North Korea*

If classical arguments proposed by Kornai[20] cannot be used as an analytical tool in the North Korean case, where can one turn? Scholarship on Chinese economic reforms paved the way more than a decade ago to defining a model for market socialism. And there have been attempts to utilize this analytic lens for the DPRK. I explain the terminology first and how it has been used in other studies, and then I consider whether it may lend itself to the case of North Korea, and if not, what other analytic tools could be available.

2.9 *Defining Market Socialism*

By "market socialism" the conventional scholarship refers to an economic system which is founded on basic market principles but allows for mixed ownership of the means of production—including state-, privately-, and jointly-owned ventures—while the communist party remains the guiding force of the economy.[21] In market socialism, the communist party is dominant in those areas deemed critical to the implementation of socialist principles and social policy. It is described as "a species of economic system which is, in a number of ways, a cross between capitalism and socialism".[22] The core tenet of market socialism is that the markets are not exclusive to capitalism, but, if directed and limited by the state, and curtailed so not to affect the political stability of the state, can be compatible with collective ownership and socialist principles.[23]

2.10 *How Does Market Socialism Work in Practice, in Countries Where it is Applied?*

The first primary feature of a market socialist economy is the retention of substantial state and collective ownership of the means of production. Where market socialism has been implemented, the conventional literature founds two such forms of ownership.[24] One is public market socialism and the other is self-managed market socialism. In the former, civilian communities control income rights in enterprises, with equal distribution of enterprise income to all citizens; in the latter, enterprise workers have both control and income rights.[25] China and Vietnam, which are characterized by market socialism through market-oriented reform, have achieved dynamic economic growth, with both the private and public sectors playing mutually reinforcing roles in the economy. Whatever specific form it takes, a market socialist system requires a dominant position of public ownership in the economy.[26]

What I have considered so far for is the definition of market socialism which has been partially explored in studies about the dynamics of Chinese economy and development.[27] The arguments proposed by these studies can be borrowed, to a degree, to inform a new vision of the current economic landscape in North Korea. In proposing Chinese implementation of market socialism as a model worthy of emulation by the DPRK, we must examine four major advantages:

1. Party-driven economic development, enabling efficient resource allocation;
2. Risk borne by the state, shifting the responsibility from the private sector to the public in cases of economic downturn and hardship;
3. Ability to manipulate financial policy, including currency; and
4. Maintenance of close links between the party and the government, permitting a higher degree of control.

Chu argues that the Chinese experience, having benefitted from these four major advantages, could be a starting point for a parallel with the North Korean case.[28] During the global financial crisis, China was able to stimulate aggregate demand more successfully than other economies. A leading factor was the fact that China had relatively small internal and external and a comparatively isolated financial sector, which overrode the destabilizing impact emanating from the collapse of the world financial order. Another reason for the Chinese government's successful stimulation of aggregate demand is the central command system that was not dismantled after economic reform. Under the supervision of the central government, the state allowed local authorities to implement infrastructure construction and other projects efficiently. The central government also exerted free-lending activities by the state-owned banks to avoid the credit crunch caused by the global financial crisis.

Granted, this very last point may be difficult to implement with North Korea, due to the absence of a central bank.[29] In a normally-functioning market economy, the role of the central bank is of crucial importance, allowing for the introduction and execution of viable monetary policy, setting of interest rates, regulation of money supply and supervision of the commercial banking industry. Without such a system, the implementation of any stable currency or reliable credit system is impossible—a serious hindrance to market reform.

2.11 *Is Market Socialism Appropriate to Defining the North Korean Case?*

In comparison with what the conventional literature highlights for the Chinese case, the North Korean approach to market socialism presents numerous peculiarities. The purpose of what outside observes refer to as "economic reform" or "opening policy"—but really are no more than mere adjustments of the same economic system—is to avoid the adverse impact that full-fledged market economic reform may have exerted, and at the same time to improve productivity and people's living standards while maintaining socialist principles. The main economic thrust is still an exclusive dominion of state, and it aims at buttressing the historical dominance of the state over the economy, rather than opening it to market economy. However, the state needs to reconcile growing discrepancies within a once-monolithic system, and the way it does so is to claim that these supposed "improvements"—if and where they are officially acknowledged—simply adapt *Juche* principles in a prolonged phase of the DPRK socialist society moving toward full-fledged communism in response to external challenges and changes in a new era.

In other words, what the DPRK government recognizes in addressing "improvements" is that these are not real changes (i.e.: irreversible or otherwise meaningful modifications of the system or any of its features); rather they are resourceful adaptations of the "creative principle" (i.e: the flexibility) of *Juche* ideology to current economic needs. In the socialist interpretation, market relations can exist in a socialist society only temporarily, as socialism is the transitional stage toward communism. Whatever improvements or adaptations the system may tolerate (as interpreted above), they are to be interpreted (thus they are propagandized by the government as) signs of developing the right form of a socialist economy; which is, the opposite of abandoning socialism in favor of a capitalist model of development.

In the DPRK's official view, the core of socialism remains intact, but in reality it coexists with a phenomenon (the *Jangmadang*) that resembles market relations. It is important to clarify that the role that markets play in the economy is, in the official view, at best supplementary, something that improves the living standards of people; it cannot be recognized as something to replace the state's role in guiding the economy.

John Everard explains in detail how the North Korean regime regards the market as evil through the speeches of Kim Jong Il.[30] They highlight how important it is for the nation to feed its people without resorting to temporary capitalistic measures like markets. "In a socialist society, the food problem should be solved by socialist means. If the party lets the people solve the food problem themselves, then only the farmers and merchants will prosper, giving rise to ego. The party will then lose its popular base and will experience meltdown as in Poland and Czechoslovakia." This speech, given by Kim Jong Il at Kim Il Sung University on 7 December, 1966, reveals the extent to which accepting markets is a testament to the failure of North Korea's ideology.

This is why in North Korea the government has not undertaken even a simple measure such as the leasing of state-owned means of production, land, and other resources to economic agents in unofficial markets. In the current ideological state of North Korea, the leadership simply cannot afford to legalize and bring to the surface economic activities that by definition undermines the integrity and efficacy of the *Juche* ideology and collectivism.

Therefore, in North Korea, state control remains the driving force, and the state intervenes exclusively. The core of the party-state system defines the nature and functioning of the North Korean politics and the parameters within which the state economic policy can be initiated and implemented and which the entire economy can move around. Therefore, regardless of their definition, either by the North Korean government itself or by outside observers, market activities are considered as supplementary to the efficiency of state-directed production and distribution, and are not intended to replace state-direction of the economy.

The following quote vividly underscores how the state negatively regards the market. In one speech in 2007, Kim Jong Il said: “The market has degenerated into a place which eats away at our style of socialism…and [is] a birthplace of all sorts of non-socialist practices”.[31]

He returned to the theme in another speech, delivered in mid-2008 (Haggard & Ryu 2010): “As we allowed a certain use of markets with respect to economic management, some people understood this as a departure from the socialism and “opening up” of the country’s economy… But this is incorrect reasoning…Markets are both home to and a hotbed for un-socialist phenomenon and capitalist traits of capitalism in the economic sectors’.[32]

To conclude this section: North Korea has never attempted market-oriented reform to transform the system to market socialism, and, as a result, profound distortions within the North Korean socioeconomic system have been precipitated.

The question remains as to how one can explain the current economic landscape of North Korea, not only as it is today but as it could be improved in the future. My analysis shows that North Korea’s approach to structural “improvements” of its own system has precipitated the distortions and dysfunctionality of the economy.

In the following sections, I dwell on analysis of the essential attributes of the North Korea economy and how attempts at improvement measures have led to severe distortions. Then, I discuss the five core elements of the system that have enabled the regime’s survival despite this dysfunctionality.

2.12 *The North Korean Approach: How the North’s Unique Approach has Affected Efforts to Improve the Economy*

Due to the partition of the Korean Peninsula, the North Korea’s political, economic and international structures differ from those of other socialist countries, despite sharing the same superficial socialist characteristics. This factor has been either misinterpreted or overlooked by the majority of studies on the North Korean economy, aside from a few exceptions.[33]

To begin, let's analyze the terminology: North Korea speaks of its economic adjustments in terms of "improvement," and never in terms of "reform." The idea of "improvement" includes some hint at innovation in economic management. Improvement in the political economy of North Korea cannot be compared in substance to the terminology used in the former Soviet Union's (*perestroika*) or Vietnam (*doi moi*) or China (lhei mao bai mao, "black cat, white cat" theory). One may compare the political slogans, but to assume that they imply the same scope and purpose of economic transformation would be erroneous.[34]

Therefore, what most foreign analysts miss when they adopt the terms "reform" and "opening" to describe the evolution of North Korean economy is that North Korea refers not to those terms but only to "improvement" (*Gaeson*) and, more recently, to the word "*silli*" (meaning "practicality").

In no way has North Korea ever accepted or hinted at the adoption of market-oriented economic reforms that were chosen by Eastern European countries and others such as China and Vietnam.[35]

2.13 The Five Core Components that Sustained the Integrity of the Regime and Ensured its Survival

Why have so many analysts wrongly predicted the impending collapse of North Korea for two decades? How has North Korea managed to survive despite its obvious insurmountable problems?

To briefly explain how North Korea managed to survive against overwhelming odds, and in spite of the numerous predicaments of its seemingly imminent demise in the 1990s, I consider following five key elements that served to safeguard the legitimacy and survival of the regime. The fading or erosion of each of these elements signals the possibility of a loss of control and an impending collapse:

1. *Ideology and Indoctrination*

The first core element of North Korean survival is the strong ideological basis of the regime. Over seven decades, through three generations of the Kim family, the leadership has been remarkably consistent in spreading the same message. The indoctrination relates not only to the cult of the Kim family as uniquely gifted to lead the country, but also to the establishment of the fictional reality whereby North Korea is a "paradise on Earth;"

also, the propaganda depicts South Korea as a destitute country, almost like a colony of the US Army. The propaganda also portrays outside powers, particularly the US, as having constant belligerent intentions towards the DPRK, to induce an atmosphere of constant military alert. The layers of indoctrination and the integrity of ideology have progressively eroded over the last two decades because of the contradictions between the prevailing socioeconomic reality and the ruling ideology. This erosion is one factor that could erode the foundations of the regime and instigate collapse if the government is unable to counterbalance it.

2. *Development of a successful nuclear program*

The government developed the nuclear program as both an instrument of national defense and a form threats (either perceived or real) to justify enormous sacrifice and labor extraction from the masses. The completion of the nuclear program announced by Kim Jong Un in 2017 after numerous ballistic tests signaled the last stage of a path that the DPRK has chosen since the 1980s to preserve the integrity of the system by: (1) boosting domestic legitimacy as a countermeasure to an already declining economy; (2) surpassing the imbalance with South Korea in defense capabilities (Seoul is protected under the US nuclear umbrella, while Pyongyang did not have such protection); and (3) making the DPRK truly independent in armaments, not having to rely on either China or Russia. The nuclear program, however, is not a card that North Korea can play anymore, after the diplomatic reconciliations of 2018–2019 with both South Korea and the US. Given that Kim Jong Un has gone to great lengths to convince other world leaders, particularly Donald Trump, that he is willing to negotiate, a return to nuclear blackmail is highly unlikely.

3. *Tools of political repression and social control*

The third element is the high level of social control over the life of individuals. This takes two forms. The first is the strict control of any unorthodox information coming from outside, or any external information that could invalidate the propaganda claims. The second is the social control. North Korea has achieved some of the highest levels of social control with a combination of physical repression, forced labour and ideological education. Equally important is the system of family unit and local neighbour control, known as *Inminban*. To put this in perspective, the ratio of political informants among the population in the DDR at the height of espionage activity for the East German secret police, the *Stasi*, was estimated to be between 1: 6 and 1: 7. In the North Korean system of *Inminban*, the ratio has been described by defectors as being 1: 3, meaning that out of a traditional family unit of two parents and one or two children, one would be certainly be engaged in surveillance of the others.[36] This system too, however, is now subject to erosion, particularly after North Korea has been put in the spotlight for this violation of human rights, with the 2014 United Nations Commission of Inquiry investigation.

4. *Grass-root marketization due to benign oversight*

The fourth pillar of survival for the regime is the fact that the leadership deliberately chose to allow and condone a phenomenon of bottom-up marketization for a number of reasons, namely: (1) It shifted the responsibility of providing economic necessities from the regime to the public; (2) it served to mitigate social and economic discontent, which was particularly strong during the Arduous March; and (3) it allowed for the survival of millions of people who would have otherwise perished, as many others did, between 1994 and 1999. Moreover, it freed the government from economic commitment towards the population, allowing it to focus on the *Seongun* (military first) policy. However, this market system does not qualify the DPRK as a market socialist system, as it still lacks independent sellers and buyers, a free marketplace with prices determined by supply and demand and a transition of ownership from the state to private hands.

5. *The emergence of a small coalition system of power support under Kim Jong Un*

Finally, in the KJU era, a new element is given by the emergence of a new class of economic and political elites, who can safeguard the survival of the Kim family in power, as long as Kim is able to guarantee their economic success and find them revenue streams. These new elites primarily consist of top-ranking officials in the military, party, and administration, including the *Donju*. They have been instrumental in consolidating the reign of Kim Jong Un so far, but this was only possible because North Korea had enough funds to keep this elite happy and well remunerated.

The grip of international sanctions, as we will see in detail in Chap. 3, has changed all this.

In the next three parts of this chapter I attempt to analyze what makes North Korea different from other socialist systems and therefore limits the analytical rigor of traditional frameworks frequently applied to transitional economies. In each part, I describe the elements of the system that have distorted so severely from traditional socialist norms.

3 The Initial Distortion of Socialism in North Korea: *Juche*, the *Suryong* System

The first deviation of the North Korean system from traditional socialism is linked to: (1) how the North Korean economy initially developed after the Korean War using socialist aid and mass mobilization campaigns, with periodical failures in centralized planning and (2) how the North Korean system grafted its own *Juche* ideology onto traditional socialism, and how, along with the *Suryong* system, this has led to a left-wing totalitarian system and unique dynastic succession.

The combination of traditional socialism with *Juche* ideology resulted in all power being transferred from the party to an absolute ruler. In accordance with the philosophy of an absolute leader and with North Korea's distinctive system of placing the party and all state organizations under the control of this leader, i.e. the core teachings of *Juche* ideology, the general population became subjects that obey the Dear Leader's orders and directions without hesitation, moving as one according to this leader's orders and even sacrificing their lives for their leader, thus establishing North Korea's own distinctive system of left wing totalitarianism.

3.1 *The Nature of the North Korean System (Extractive vs. Inclusive)*

The North Korean system was conceived from its inception to be *extractive* rather than *inclusive* in nature. What does this mean? Here we will address the concept briefly, but a more detailed discussion can be found in Chap. 3.

This feature is not unique to North Korea. Every socialist system, based on the collective ownership of the means of production, is designed to be extractive. The feature of collectivization itself is conducive to the extraction of labor, goods and services with the state having the role of sole supplier and sole buyer, as well as being the sole catalyst of the labor force. In other words, collectivization creates the necessary environment for exploitation.

However, as the North Korean economy differs in many features from other socialist economies, so does its system of extraction. The extractive nature of the North Korean system placed extra emphasis on the completion of extravagant projects of grandeur (such as the model city of Pyongyang, the Ryukyong Hotel, the monuments to the Kim family, the new streets dedicated to scientists, the Arirang games, and so forth) and the prioritization of heavy industry for military purposes, to the detriment of agriculture and light industry and ultimately to the stagnation of economic growth.

Furthermore, under the Kim Jong Un leadership, propaganda projects have not only accelerated in scope, but also changed in their political nature. The system of a small coalition is based on the "leasing" of lucrative activities to the rising class of *nouveau riches*, known as *Donju*.[37] Entrusting individuals with showcase projects allowed Kim Jong Un to buy their loyalty, and enabled the *Donju* to find sources of income based on labor extractions—for instance, by using the army as manpower.

3.2 Defining Features of the System

First, let us summarize the aspects that are similar to other socialist systems, in the foundations of the North Korean system. After gaining power in 1945, Kim Il Sung formed a temporary government on February 8, 1946, nationalizing all major production means, including major corporations, transportation, banks, mines, coal pits and forests, and confiscating land from their owners to be distributed to farmers at no cost. In all the editions of the Socialist Constitution of the Democratic People's Republic of Korea, proclaimed on April 13, 2012, the North Korean government provides explicit provisions concerning the ownership of production means. According to Chap. 2, Article 20 of the Constitution, "Means of production in the Democratic People's Republic of Korea are owned by the State and social cooperative organizations". Article 21 defines the scope and subject of state-ownership by stipulating that "There is no limit to the scope of ownership by the State. All natural resources, railroads, air transportation, communications agencies, and major factories, corporate sites, ports, banks can only be owned by the State". It is worth remembering that when I examine the formation process of economic systems in socialist states, it is the dominant ideology that leads to the nationalization of all production means, rather than the opposite. This implies that any attempt at the privatization of production means—a key step towards systemic reforms of any economy—necessitates *a priori* a change in the dominant ideology that regulates and oversees the socialist economy system.

Second, let us look at what sets the DPRK apart from all other socialist systems: its ideology and system of leadership. Rather than self-reliance, *Juche* ideology was used to consolidate the DPRK's unique system of dynastic succession within a communist dictatorship, which is different from how communism evolved in China or Russia. When Kim Il Sung was pressured to choose a side of communism, either China or Russia, due to the antagonistic Sino-Russian relationship in the Stalin era, Kim adopted *Juche*, which is a combination of socialism and DPRK nepotism-based totalitarianism.

4 The Collapse of the Soviet Union and the Second Distortion of the System: Dysfunctional Marketization of the North Korean Economy

The second major distortion of the socialist system in North Korea developed in consequence of the crisis that since 1990 has affected the DPRK. The socialist collapse has ushered in profound consequences on North Korea. The most evident manifestations of this distortion are reflected in the grass-root marketization of the economy, known as the *Janmadang*, and the deliberate acquiescence of state-owned means of production for use in the private sector. No longer able to provide the minimum amount of food needed for its population, the regime began applying a "benign oversight" approach to these unsanctioned activities. Instead of confronting economic crisis or introducing reforms to rectify the situation, the DPRK has implemented passive, cosmetic measures—reform within the system rather than of the system. Proof of this are the failed attempts at improving the system from within with two sets of measures: the July 1st 2002 measures, and the currency reform of 2009. In both cases however, the government's approach to reform has been passive—that is, responsive rather than active.

4.1 The Shock of the Soviet Collapse and the Arduous March

Before going into the details of the consequences of the Soviet collapse on North Korea, it is necessary to illustrate the nature of the crisis of the 1990s and particularly what is commonly referred to as the "Arduous March". I will briefly explain how the 1990s crisis unfolded and then examine how this influenced the field of North Korean studies.

In 1995, for the first time in its history, North Korea, requested assistance from the international community. After the demise of its first leader, Kim Il Sung, in 1994, and due to a combination of domestic and international factors, the DPRK faced a socioeconomic crisis in all sectors of society as well as state institutions.[38] Per capita income decreased sharply from $2,460 in 1991 to $719 in 1995, while exports declined from $2 billion to a meager $800 million. As a result of famine caused by the stunted agricultural sector, further aggravated by harsh climatic conditions, an estimated 600,000 to 2 million North Koreans had perished by 1998.

The factors contributing to this socioeconomic crisis are worth summarizing here. In 1991, the DPRK had lost its main ally, the Soviet Union, while in 1993 China had started to demand payments at regular market rates for oil and fuel which had until then been provided at very low prices.[39] As the international scenario changed rapidly from the early 1990s, the DPRK, which during the Cold War had become heavily dependent on subsidized trade with members of the Eastern socialist bloc, found itself with no economic safety net. The shortage of energy directly affected the agriculture system, as this was almost entirely reliant on chemical fertilizers and mechanized irrigation.[40] With diminishing amounts of food, the effectiveness of the Public Distribution System (PDS) that regulated the allocation of basic goods decreased gradually, forcing the population to seek alternative means of subsistence. Housewives, factory workers, doctors, nurses, teachers and students had to fend for themselves to secure food and heating material during winter.[41]

The conventional literature on the economic crisis of the 1990s points to the fact that food deprivation, energy shortages and overall economic collapse came as a shock to many North Koreans. The situation, certainly, was aggravated by adverse climatic events (floods, hailstorms and droughts between 1994 and 1998), as well as by external pressures from accumulating international debts[42] although the conventional scholarship does ascribe a degree of the crisis to economic mismanagement. The PDS did not collapse altogether, and its operational status varied between different provinces; however, the fact that the general population could not rely on the PDS as it had done in the past, coupled with the growing shortages of energy, meant that regular working activities (in schools, hospitals and factories) either slowed down or had to be interrupted (as it was the case in many schools and universities) to secure essential goods.[43]

Particular facets of this period in the North Korean economy should be highlighted. From the 1990s and throughout the first decade of the 2000s, the DPRK witnessed the following alterations of its inner balance:

Bottom-up, unofficially sanctioned marketization has taken place as the state acquiesces to leasing the means of production and other state-owned resources for private use, including the selling and buying of privately-produced goods and services. By the term "privatization," a non-specialist reader may understand two different things. One is the appropriation of state-owned enterprises for private use (an "abandonment of socialism", in practice) as it happens in North Korea today. The other is the "private ownership of the means of production" (which characterizes a standard market economy). Yoon argues that since 1992 the DPRK has witnessed a destabilization of its Public Distribution System (PDS); according to Yoon, the years since 1992 present a general case of deviation of socialism that can be found in any socialist countries (socialist market), backed by allowing unauthorized, unofficial business entities to operate, thus breeding corruption.[44] Yoon ascribes this to the emergence of favorable conditions for institutionalizing the deviation that provided radical expansion of markets. In the DPRK, up to today, this change did not accompany large-scale selling of assets, and capital transactions remain small.

To build on this argument, I would add that "privatization" is different from "de-nationalisation". What happens in North Korea under Kim Jong Un is a process of benign oversight: the acquiescence by the state to private entities to use land, mines, fishing license and trade. This phenomenon is tolerated but still officially unauthorized. This means the state offers an unofficial social contract with a few groups of people—namely the *Donju*, high level party members and public officials, and a few diplomats.[45] As this process is still illegal—in that the means of production are still owned by the state—three consequences arise: (1) no security is guaranteed in these parallel economic activities, and consequently no accumulation of capital which can be made otherwise possible (under a normal market economy) through monetary policy, domestic currency control, taxes, loans, creation of a stock market, interest rate policy, investments, and trade (through openness); (2) no legalization of ownership, leasing, inheritance, buying or selling; and (3) high transaction cost due to bribery at every stage of contract.

This is coupled with the progressive erosion (but not yet collapse) of bureaucratic control. The current North Korean economy can best be described as having fallen into a quagmire, helplessly bogged down in the inherent contradictions and flaws of the previous Soviet Union system it modeled itself after. To understand how the North Korean economy has developed such irreconcilable contradictions within its system, I must analyze the three major economic policies adopted and implemented by the North Korean regime. The following is an explanation of three key policies which have mainly contributed to the collapse of the North Korean economy.

4.2 *Attempts at Improvements Within the System, or "cosmetic reforms"*

The first policy is the implementation of reform within the system, instead of reform of the system, to cure the systemic contradictions and flaws within the socialist, Soviet-modeled economic system of North Korea, a decision which further exacerbated contradictory and irrational aspects within the North Korean economy. During the early 1990s, when the Soviet Union and other communist nations within the Eastern Bloc were exploring ways to reform their socialistic economies as market systems, North Korea decided to preserve the centrally-planned, Soviet-style economy. Following the great famine North Korea endured in the mid-1990s—the "Arduous March"—North Korea decided to carry out a series of measures in 2002 that aimed at rectifying the critical contradictions and flaws within its system.

These measures amounted to an attempt at reform within the system and became known as the "July 1 Measures," named after the announcement date. The major goals of the July 1 Measures were to readjust the prices of goods to a realistic level, implement an independent profit system, distribute profits according to productivity, and expand the autonomy of the management of state enterprises. The basic features of North Korea's July 1 Measures were largely identical to the economic reform carried out by Walter Ulbricht in East Germany from 1963 to 1965 (also called the "New Economic System"), and that carried out by Mikhail Gorbachev from 1985 to 1991 in the Soviet Union.[46]

A clear example that abundantly illustrates the failure of this reform was the soaring inflation that followed North Korea's reforms. Directly after the July 1 Measures, the market price for rice was around 45 won per kilogram, while the market exchange rate for U.S. dollars maintained a level of approximately 150 won per dollar. By September 2009 the market price for rice had jumped to 2,400 won per kilogram and U.S. dollars were being traded at 3,800 won in the foreign exchange market. Thus, during the seven years following implementation of the July 1 Measures in 2002, the price of rice had multiplied by 53 times and the market exchange rate for U.S. dollars had risen by 25 times. In other words, rice prices had undergone an annual average increase of 750 percent for seven consecutive years, while the foreign exchange rate had jumped by 360 percent during the same period. The hyperinflation and bi-polarization of income caused by the July 1 Measures would eventually lead to the currency reform carried out by North Korea in November 2009, which will be further examined later in this chapter.

4.3 Socioeconomic Consequences of Importing Necessities Rather than Capital Goods

The second policy that accelerated the collapse of the North Korean economy was the state's decision to limit import of capital goods, leading to the demise of North Korea's manufacturing sector. Following the collapse of socialistic systems in the Soviet Union and other communist nations in the Eastern Bloc, with which North Korea enjoyed a close economic relationship at the time, North Korea decided to import necessities, including consumer goods, instead of capital goods to promote macroeconomic stability in its economy. Such limits on the import of capital goods effectively accelerated the collapse of North Korea's manufacturing sector. While other factors contributed to this collapse—for instance, the failure of North Korea to integrate with the world economy through market-oriented reform and opening, leading to electricity shortages, disruptions in the supply of raw material input, and the state's production-related technology falling behind—it was this deliberate limitation placed on the import of capital goods that directly caused the manufacturing sector to collapse.

The collapse of the Soviet Union in the early 1990s and other communism regimes with which North Korea enjoyed strong economic ties, as discussed earlier, delivered a severe blow to North Korea's foreign trade.

The fall in its overall volume of trade with these nations also had an effect on North Korea's import of capital goods. As has been pointed out by Eberstadt, the reason that the ratio of capital goods from North Korea's total trade volume import has continued to fall since 1990 lies in how the states has deliberately lowered the ratio of production goods from its imports.[47]

Entering 2010, North Korea's foreign trade began to recover to levels seen prior to 1990 and has continued to increase rapidly. However, the ratio of capital goods to necessities has fallen even lower from its overall amount of imports. This rapid rise in North Korea's foreign trade is mostly due to its trade with China. In 2014, North Korea's trade with China rose over 90% of its total trade. Together with such a concentration in North Korea's trade, another pronounced trend has been that most of the state's imports are basic commodities such as crude oil, as well as TVs, mobile phones, or trucks, necessities that are mainly imported from China, while coal, iron ore and other mineral products are exported exclusively to China. Such an imbalance in North Korea's exports to China, and its reliance on iron ore or other mineral products which require little technology, and thus have lower-value added, representing a low level of national competitiveness, has continued to become even more pronounced. Over the period of 2008 to 2012, the percentage of goods from among North Korea's exports to China rose from 25 to 57.5%.

Due to the decline of the manufacturing sector, as a result of harsh international sanctions, the economy has experienced a considerable decline of the GDP of −4.1% noted in 2018, with exports plummeting by 90% to a mere $200 million. Due to the sizeable trade deficit, which has reached $2 billion and continues to grow, the state operating fund has dwindled as the regime tries to make up the difference. Compounded with an estimated food shortage of 1.4 million metric tonnes of grain, North Korea is even more reliant on trade with China than ever, and prospects for 2019 are just as dismal.[48]

Such a concentration on the import of basic necessities, and not on capital goods, incapacitated North Korea's manufacturing sector, inevitably leading to the state's decision to discontinue centralized economic planning. North Korea stopped establishing detailed economic plans after the last Seven Year Plan that began in 1987 and ended in 1993, becoming the only socialist nation to give up on a centralized and planned economic structure.

This collapse in the centralized economic planning carried out by the state also disrupted the public distribution system of goods, in which state corporations produced goods and either sold them at government-approved prices or supplied them through official distribution networks. Due to the disintegration of the manufacturing sector, which severely disrupted the circular flow of income and output, government expenditure exceeded revenue. As the deficit continued to grow, the DPRK answered by simply printing more currency, triggering hyperinflation.

The people were left with no other choice than to rely on the black markets, or *Jangmadang*, for food and other basic needs. Today there are more than 380 *Jangmadang* across the nation, accounting for more than half of the gross national product. The emergence of an unofficial economy within North Korea has also caused an extreme bi-polarization of income between merchants engaging in the unofficial economic sector and laborers employed in the state-sector. This progression of events also led to the state's decision to implement currency reform in November 2009.

4.4 *The 2009 Currency Reform*

The currency reform implemented in November of 2009 represents the last attempt by the North Korean government to suppress the continuous growth of the unofficial economy due to hyperinflation, and to restore the previous socialist economic order to the country. In 2009, when the health of Chairman Kim Jong Il continued to deteriorate and succession by Kim Jong Un seemed certain, the first priority was to reestablish the paralyzed socialist economic order. As can be inferred from official statements issued on the 2009 currency reform the measure's main objective was to address the severe income disparity between the state and private sectors, as well as to restore the socialist order. On December 4, 2009, the Chosun Shinbo stated the main purposes of the currency reform as:

1. The alleviation of inflation by observing monetary overhang;
2. The restoration of planned economic order through stronger state distribution networks;
3. Protection for the welfare of state employees;
4. Increased purchasing power; and
5. Suppression of foreign currency use.

The regime's true motivation, of course, was the transfer of wealth from the hands of individuals to the state—a form of forced taxation. To realize the aforementioned policy goals, the government placed into action an extreme set of measures to reform the currency regime, which can be summarized as follows.

- The exchange rate between new and old currency was set at 1:100 (for instance, a 1000-won note in the old currency could be exchanged for a 10-won note in the new currency).
- Each individual could exchange a maximum of 150,000 won (approximately 45–60 dollars) in cash and 300,000 won (approximately 90–120 dollars) in their bank account.
- Despite this, the salary of all state-employed laborers remained identical to pre-reform levels, increasing 100-fold the wages of state-employed laborers.[49]

As a result of these reform measures, an enormous amount of cash assets belonging to individual residents lost its value instantaneously and was reclaimed by the government. Directly after the currency reform, the market price for rice was artificially pegged at 23 won per kilogram and the market exchange rate for dollars was set at 38 won per U.S. dollar. The currency reform instigated precisely the opposite effect of its intended goals and triggered catastrophic consequences that led to the North Korean economy falling into an inescapable quagmire.

4.5 *The Consequences of the Currency Reform*

The 2009 the currency reform caused three major problems:

1. Hyperinflation; uncontrollable rise in inflation rates;
2. Persistent income disparity between of merchants employed in the unofficial economic sector and laborers working in the official economic sector;
3. Overwhelming circulation of foreign currency, namely through dollarization, as a means of payment for the transaction of services and goods;

4.5.1 *Hyperinflation*

The currency reform of 2009 exacerbated the existing inflation caused by the July 1 Measures of 2002, leading to a state of hyperinflation. While the market price of rice was artificially limited to 23 won per kilogram directly after the reform measures, this price had skyrocketed to 240 won by February 4th of the following year, amounting to an increase of over 1000% in a mere three months. The price of rice and the exchange rate for U.S. dollars has continued to rise at a rapid pace ever since. In 2013, three years after the currency reform, a kilogram of rice rose to 5,000 won and the market exchange rate for U.S. dollars to 8,000 won. In effect, the price of rice has risen by 217-fold (an annual increase of 720% on average), and the exchange rate for U.S. dollars by 211-times (annual average increase of 700%), over a three-year period.[50] This state of hyperinflation has led to North Korean residents shunning the domestic currency, accelerating dollarization and, thus, further widening the income disparity between merchants engaged in the unofficial sector and laborers in the state sector.

4.5.2 *Persistent Income Disparity between the Unofficial Market Sector and the State Sector*

Continual hyperinflation in North Korea caused an extreme income imbalance, with the *Donju* and merchants in the unofficial sectors of the economy on one end of the spectrum, and the laborers employed by state organizations on the other. The following episode brings into sharp contrast the income disparity between laborers in the state sector and merchants in the unofficial sector, including money lenders (namely *Donju*). In 2014, Simon Mundy, a correspondent for the *Financial Times*, reported on his interview with Yang Gang-jin, a North Korean intercity truck driver on a family outing to the newly-opened Mansudae Fountain Park. In the interview, Mr. Yang, shares his experience of paying an entry fee of 20,000 won per person (approximately five times the average monthly wage of a North Korean laborer), and enjoying hamburgers and beer in the price range of 10,000 won, which comes to around twice the monthly wages of an ordinary laborer.[51] This example highlights the gross contradiction between those employed formally in the state sector and those employed in the private sector. Another illuminating episode of the growing income gap in North Korea is provided by Andrei Lankov in his book, *The Real North Korea*. Lankov relates how Ms. Young, a North Korean woman, turns a profit selling used women clothing made in China at one of the

Jangmadang. A technician working at a state corporation, Ms. Young pays 40 dollars a month in bribes to her supervisor, or 20 times her monthly salary of 2 dollars, to exempt her from her official duties and allow her to work at the *Jangmadang*.[52] These real-life examples illustrate the great income disparity that has grown between merchants working in the unofficial sectors and laborers employed by the state. This bi-polarization damages the legitimacy of the traditional North Korean socialist system and erodes the roots of its official ruling ideology.

4.5.3 *Overwhelming Circulation of Foreign Currency for Transactions of Services and Goods*

Following the currency reform of 2009, the use of foreign currency (U.S. dollars, Chinese yuan, euros) instead of the domestic currency has become much more prevalent in North Korea, both as a medium of exchange and as a means of storing value. The currency reform carried out in September 2009 in effect reabsorbed the majority of the people's lifetime savings back into the state's coffers. Naturally, the reform was met with growing resentment and distrust on the part of the people. "According to reports, Pak Nam-ki, the party official who was known to have led the currency reform, took responsibility for the failure of the reform and was summarily executed."[53] North Korean residents avoid storing cash in the domestic currency, and no one entrusts their money to the state bank due to mistrust in the government. Foreign cash accounts for 50 percent to 80 percent of transactions in private markets.[54]

According to an April 2013 analysis by the Samsung Economic Research Institute in Seoul, the total amount of hard currency in circulation within North Korea is estimated at around $2 billion, which amounts to 10.5% of the country's gross domestic product in 2013. The composition of these foreign currency holdings is 50% U.S. dollars, 40% Chinese Yuan and 10% Euros.[55] According to Marcus Noland, a North Korea expert, "It's been a tug of war for 20 years, where the state would like to get control of the economy…but it just doesn't have the capacity to do any of those things," he said. "It just makes it harder and harder for them to govern. Nobody wants what they're selling".[56] As the majority of transactions occurring in the unofficial economic sector takes place in foreign currency, the state has lost its capability to efficiently manage and control the economy.[57]

5 The Third Distortion of the System: The Detrimental Effects of International Sanctions and the Rise of the *Donju*

Since the North Korean economy has been subject to international sanctions, the system has attributed to further, pervasive distortion of its original socialist roots. The growing burden of international sanctions—since the first missile test of 2006 and the rise to power of Kim Jong Un in 2012—has taken a heavy toll on the economy. Sanctions have drastically reduced export revenues, and accordingly, the ability to import from China. The system has also applied increasing pressure on all its social strata, further squeezing the majority of its population in favor of small, elite groups. The regime lost it control over the economy through the rise of the unofficial sector, *Jangmadang*, and the exacerbations of international sanctions, causing Kim Jong Un to grow increasingly dependent on the support of a "small coalition;" a system of elite power sharing.

5.1 *The Detrimental Effects of UNSC-imposed Sanctions*

The most detrimental social and economic consequences have come as a direct impact of the application of threat through harsh international sanctions from the international community, the impact of which can be measured with a series of 14 indicators, described in the passage to follow: (1) increase in the current account deficit; (2) decrease of GNP (the final value of all goods and services produced by the citizens of one country); (3) shortage of food supply; (4) increased unemployment (5) escalating foreign exchange rate; (6) rapid dollarization; (7) hyperinflation; (8) income disparity between unofficial and socialist sectors; (9) breakdown of bureaucratic controlling mechanisms, including (9a) undermined ideological indoctrination; (9b) breakdown of the central rationing system; (10) exploitation of domestic servants and overseas workers; (11) human rights violations; (12) dissemination of unauthorized information; (13) criminal punishment and executions; and (14) mass defection.

After harsh bans implemented in 2017 on coal, mineral, textile, and seafood exports, annual revenue has been cut by over $2 billion. Energy products, including coal and minerals, together with textiles have composed the nation's top two exports since 2011, and they alone have accounted for a loss of more than US $1.705 billion upon implementation of the UNSC resolution 2371 and 2375. In the past, North Korea's saving grace has been China's reluctance to crack down on unauthorized trade, but in recent years China has faithfully abided by its commitment to UNSC sanctions, reducing imports from North Korea by 86.1% at the beginning of 2018, and likewise cutting their imports from the nation by 34%.

In spite of some illicit export channels, revenue has continued to drop accordingly, limiting the outflow of goods from the isolated nation and obstructing the inflow of foreign currency. Compounded with the loss of labor remittances from overseas workers, projected to generate over $500 million annually for the regime, this ongoing deterioration of revenue has a detrimental effect on the state's ever-widening current account deficit. Unable to sustain this deficit, the regime is already faced with colossal shortages of oil, machinery, and raw goods—a perilous chain effect set off by diminishing exports. The backbone of the centralized economy, the manufacturing sector, subsequently is experiencing an agonizing downturn as sources of fuel, equipment, and materials diminish. Reduced coal output due to inability to restore flooded coal mines to functional use and a shortage of the necessary machinery are worsening the energy shortage, impacting other industries and creating a negative feedback loop that devastates levels of domestic production and inflict long-term consequences on the trajectory of the North Korean GDP. As consumption and investment crumble, rates of unemployment rapidly increasing, laying the groundwork for a wave of social unrest.

As income from production and exports wane, the regime will be left with a growing gap between actual state revenue and government expenditures. Forced to finance massive operating funds—particularly, the salaries of public servants and the upkeep of its prohibitively expensive military—the state will be forced to respond by printing more currency. As the economy is flooded by newly-minted won, inflation will soar. Retailers will react by pulling inventory off of shelves in order to sell for higher prices in won at a later date. The value of the won will nosedive, leading to a full-scale currency crisis.

Throughout Kim Jong-un's leadership, the black market exchange rates for rice and foreign currencies have remained remarkably stable. This stability in the face of tumultuous foreign trade suggests heavy-handed government intervention. However, as inflation begins to rise, foreign currency reserves dry up, and supplies of both homegrown and imported rice diminish, the government will no longer be able to support its currency, and thusly the foreign exchange rate will increase. The use of foreign currency over the won further props up the unofficial market sector and accelerate growing income disparity between the state and private sectors. Unlike advanced market economies, North Korea is incapable of introducing macroeconomic policies to alleviate the effects of acute destabilization due to the decentralization of its dysfunctional central planning system.

As the gap between the regime's revenue and expenditure widens, it will grow progressively desperate for means of financing its operating fund. Inevitably, this will lead to an increase in the extortion of overseas workers, the majority of whom live under poor conditions and retain meager cuts of their earned salaries. Likewise, exploitation of domestic labor will escalate as government officials squeeze the civilian sector for income.

In the latter half of 2017, the North Korean regime lowered its daily rations quota from 400 grams of food per person to 300 grams, falling considerably short of its self-imposed goal of 573 grams per day, and measuring at exactly half of the UN's global nutritional standard of 600 grams per day. This substantial cut is indicative of the grim condition of the nation's agriculture systems, which for five consecutive years have come up nearly 500,000 metric tons short of the minimum output required to meet its self-imposed goal, according to figures supplied by the Rural Development Administration of South Korea. This shortage will lead to inevitable famine and collapse of the central rationing system, as prolonged drought in the spring and summer of 2017 caused the loss of another 1.7% of the total harvest of rice, maize, and potatoes to be consumed in the 2018 grain year.

With human rights violations mounting and systems of bureaucratic control disintegrating, social unrest and widespread discontent will promptly follow, while rates of defection will climb sharply, already reaching approximately 1,127 in 2017 despite intense measures to consolidate security, especially along the Sino-DPRK border. Once mobility expands, information freely circulates, and the risk of staying behind outweighs that of defection, the massive outpour of North Korean defectors will prove to be a fatal blow to the deteriorating security of the regime.

5.2 *The Rise of the* Donju *and the Vulnerability of the North Korean Economy*

Another major consequence of these deteriorating socioeconomic conditions is the modification to the class system (the *Seongbun*). This is exemplified by two phenomena. The first is the rise of *nouveaux riches*, now an integral part of mainstream economic activities.[58] The *Donju* class is at the center of these unofficial economic activities and operates by orbiting around the state, but not under its direct control or by any official affiliation.[59] The second important aspect of societal change deriving from the unofficial economy in the DPRK is the shift in gender perspectives.[60] Since the mid- to late 1980s women in North Korea have engaged in various kinds of extra work, apart from their official occupation and traditional roles in households.[61] Particularly during the period of the food crisis,[62] women took the responsibility for family welfare, as trade in the markets became the main source of survival.[63]

The loss of state capability to manage and control the national economy, which foreshadows an impending economic disaster. With the loss of its capability to control the economy, the state has become unable to formulate and carry out any macroeconomic policy that aims to stabilize the economy. The above mentioned July 1 Measures, currency reform of 2009, and other policy measures taken by the nation's leadership have not only failed to improve the efficiency of the economy, but have further exacerbated its contradictions and flaws.

The impending economic disaster threatening the nation, in the midst of the state's loss of its capacity to manage and control the economy, will likely become a critical test of Chairman Kim's capabilities in crisis management. Why is that? The North Korean economy is exceptionally vulnerable to external and internal shocks. This is due to two key factors: (1) overwhelming dependence on China; and (2) the backwards agricultural sector.

China is the most important trading partner for North Korea, accounting for over 90% of its total trade volume. For six straight years, beginning in 2009, China has recorded declining production in manufacturing and overall GDP growth. According to a *Financial Times* report on October 14, 2015, the China Caixin manufacturing purchasing managers' index recorded the lowest output in 78 months.[64] Any change in the economic or political conditions in China will have major, adverse effects on North Korea's economy. North Korea's trade volume with China stood at a total of $6.89 billion in 2014, with $2.84 billion in exports and $4.02 billion in imports. Together with a rise in trade dependence on China, from 89.1% in 2013 to 90.1% in 2014, North Korea's trade deficit rose to $1.18 billion. The fall in North Korea's exports to China will further exacerbate its chronic trade deficit and inevitably decrease imports of food and other basic necessities essential to macroeconomic stability.

The second important factor that reveals the susceptibility of the North Korean economy is the agricultural sector's backwardness, particularly its vulnerability to natural disasters, as demonstrated by the 1.4 million metric ton grain shortage recorded in 2018. According to the UN Food and Agricultural Organization, rice production has fallen by 12% and the production of wheat and barley by an astonishing 30%.[65] According to recent estimates, the total grain production has fallen by 600,000 tons from 2013 levels, 300,000 tons in rice and 300,000 in wheat and barley combined. According to a 2012 report by the United Nations, over 25% of North Korea's children under the age of five suffer from malnutrition. Together with limitations on food imports, the fall in grain production North Korea as witnessed in 2015 serves as a compelling factor for further economic difficulties North Korea will likely endure as output falls due to declining labor productivity stemming from the malnutrition of the population, thus emanating social unrest.

6 Conclusion

In conclusion, it must be reiterated that the idiosyncratic, unique quagmire of the North Korean economy has set the country so far apart from the experience of other socialist states that the adoption of market-oriented reform and opening is hindered. Acknowledging that, until 1991, the DPRK system managed to muddle through despite the dysfunctional economy, the regime is now entering a new phase, plagued by extreme distortion that stems from both the disintegration of the Soviet Union and other communist nations in the Eastern Bloc in the 1990s, as well as the harsh economic sanctions facing the contemporary regime.

Having refused to undertake viable reform of the system itself, unlike the experience of other socialist and post-socialist states that either transformed or collapsed, North Korea opted to implement, rather, a number of cosmetic changes and marketization through the acquiescence of state-owned enterprises for private use, essentially creating a distorted economy—one which has ensured their survival thus far despite its innumerable mutilations of the original planned economy. Through the application of benign oversight (perhaps more aptly termed "benign neglect") to the appropriation of state owned means of production for unofficial market activity, the Kim Jong Un regime has managed to survive.

Thus, we can argue that the condition of the contemporary North Korean economy is incomparable to that of any other socialist state, past or present, and point, in turn, to their history as the root of this inimitability. The DPRK's fundamental identity as rival to its capitalist southern neighbor has dictated every aspect of political and economic decision-making since its inception. This bipolar division between the North and South has created such a dire contrast in prosperity that, unless Kim Jong Un can rectify this disparity to vitalize the economy and dismantle the nuclear weapons program, the regime will soon face collapse and inevitable absorption by the South, which is not the most effective means of achieving unification.

With an economy crippled by internationally-imposed sanctions and the myriad economic and social repercussions to ensue, the question lingers: how long can this distorted economy be sustained without instigating upheaval and undermining the legitimacy of the Kim Jong Un regime? The analysis to follow in Chap. 3, I believe, will test the hypothesis that the North Korean system is on the brink of calamity unless Kim Jong Un can make the bold and audacious decision to trade nuclear weapons for modernization, undertaking radical market-oriented economic reform and opening.

Notes

1. Fifield, Anna. 2019. *The Great Successor: The Secret Rise and Rule of Kim Jong Un*. New York: John Murray.
2. Armstrong, Charles King. 2005. *The Two Koreas*. London: Routledge; Eberstadt, Nicholas. 2009. *The North Korean Economy*. London: Routledge. p. 78; Kim, Byung-Yeon, Kim, Suk Jin, & Lee, Keun. 2007. "Assessing the Economic Performance of North Korea, 1954–1989: Estimates and Growth Accounting Analysis." *Journal of Comparative Economics* 35: 564–582.
3. MOU. 2019. "Weekly Report on North Korea." Retrieved from https://www.unikorea.go.kr/eng_unikorea/relations/infoNK/weekly/; OECD. 2019. "GDP." Retrieved from https://data.oecd.org/korea.htm
4. By 'marketization' I refer to a bottom-up process, competently autonomous and spontaneous, that began in the aftermath of the humanitarian crisis of the 1990s and the famine that ensued. As I explain further down in the chapter, the process is not related to any top-down decision or policy by the North Korean government, which ultimately chose to reluctantly accept this phenomenon as the lesser of many evils, because the state apparatus and particularly the public distribution system was on the verge of collapsing, therefore citizens could no longer rely on it for food security and survival.

5. In this book I take for granted that the reader has a basic understanding of the two main economic systems in place today: capitalism and socialism, and their major variations. Although a detailed disquisition of these terms goes beyond the scope and purpose of my work here, it is important to clarify that in this book I look beyond the traditional systems. Originally, Adam Smith and Karl Marx presented two ideal economic types: the 'free market economy' of capitalism and the 'planned command economy' of communism. In time, there have been developments of numerous mixed systems since states and markets play varying roles in different countries. We can witness this in capitalist economies within the same type of political economic system, where important variations exist such as those between the United States, Italy, Great Britain, Japan and Germany. See: Stradiotto, Gary & Guo, Sujian. 2007a. "Market Socialism in North Korea: A Comparative Perspective." *Journal of the Asia Pacific Economy* 12 (2): 188–214.
6. Although a full disquisition of economic terminology (private property, property rights, privatization and collectivization) lies beyond the scope of this chapter it is necessary to provide at least a condensed explanation. As a noun, *Privatization* indicates "the transfer of a business, industry, or service from public to private ownership and control." See: Collins Business English Dictionary. n.d. Retrieved from https://www.collinsdictionary.com/dictionary/english/privatize. The word privatization may however mean different things depending on the context in which it is used. It can mean moving something from the public sphere into the private sphere, but it may also be used to describe something that was always private, but heavily regulated, which becomes less regulated through a process of deregulation. The term may also be used descriptively for something that has always been private, but could be public in other jurisdictions. There are also private entities that may perform public functions. These entities could also be described as privatized. Privatization may mean the government sells state-owned businesses to private interests, but it may also be discussed in the context of the privatization of services or government functions, where private entities are tasked with the implementation of government programs or performance of government services. Gillian E. Metzger has written that: "Private entities [in the US] provide a vast array of social services for the government; administer core aspects of government programs; and perform tasks that appear quintessentially governmental, such as promulgating standards or regulating third-party activities." Metzger mentions an expansion of privatization that includes health and welfare programs, public education, and prisons. See: Metzger, Gillian E. 2003. "Privatization as Delegation." *Center for Constitutional Governance* 103 (1367): 1369. *Private Ownership*—usually defined as *Private Property* instead indicates the

"Tangible and intangible things owned by individuals or firms over which their owners have exclusive and absolute legal rights, such as land, buildings, money, copyrights, patents, etc. Private property can be transferred only with its owner's consent, and by due process such as sale or gift." See: Collins Business English Dictionary. n.d. Retrieved from https://www.collinsdictionary.com/dictionary/english/private-property. Private property is a legal designation for the ownership of property by non-governmental legal entities. Private property is distinguishable from public property, which is owned by a state entity; and from collective (or cooperative) property, which is owned by a group of non-governmental entities. Private property can be either personal property (consumption goods) or capital goods. Private property is a legal concept defined and enforced by a country's political system. Finally, the terms Right to Use indicates "A personal servitude conferring a specified use of an estate that is less than full enjoyment". See: Merriam-Webster. n.d. Retrieved from https://www.merriam-webster.com/legal/right%20of%20use. *Easement* represents a similar legal concept: "the right to use the real property of another for a specific purpose. The easement is itself a real property interest, but legal title to the underlying land is retained by the original owner for all other purposes. Typical easements are for access to another property, (redundantly often stated "access and egress," since entry and implication of exodus are over the same path), for utility or sewer lines both under and above ground, use of spring water, entry to make repairs on a fence or slide area, drive cattle across, and other uses." Easements can be created by a deed to be recorded just like any real property interest.

7. The law of value (German: *Wertgesetz*) is a central concept in Karl Marx's critique of political economy first expounded in his polemic The Poverty of Philosophy (1847) against Pierre-Joseph Proudhon with reference to David Ricardo's economics Generally, it refers to a regulative principle of the economic exchange of the products of human work, namely that the relative exchange-values of those products in trade, usually expressed by money-prices, are proportional to the average amounts of human labor-time which are socially necessary to produce them. See: Oishi, Takahisi. 2001. *The unknown Marx: reconstructing a unified perspective*. Foreword by Terrell Carver. London: Pluto Press; Eaton, John. 1963. *Political Economy: A Marxist Textbook*. Reprinted 1970. p. 29.
8. In 1922, Professor L. Von Mises of the Austrian School of Economics pointed out this concept in his paper "Socialism: An Economic and Social Analysis".
9. Boettke, Peter J. 1990. *The Political Economy of Soviet Socialism: the Formative Years, 1918–1928*. New York: Springer Science+Business Media New York.

10. Hayek, Friedrich A. 1980. "The Uses of Knowledge in Society." *Individualism and Economic Order*. Chicago: University of Chicago Press, p. 80.
11. Von Mises, Ludwig. 1922. "Socialism: An Economic and Social Analysis." *Austrian School of Economics.*
12. Hayek, Friedrich A. 1944. *The Road to Serfdom*, University of Chicago Press, pp. 91.
13. Hayek, Friedrich A. 1944. *The Road to Serfdom*, University of Chicago Press, pp. 92.
14. Although the proportion of marketization in the country's GDP is now estimated to be around 50%, meaning that it is not just nominal but real, this is insufficient to qualify the North Korean economy as one which is in any way transitioning or changing as other former socialist systems did.
15. Kornai, János. 1980. "The dilemmas of a socialist economy: the Hungarian experience." *Cambridge Journal of Economics* 4: 147–157; Kornai, János. 1992. *The Socialist System: The Political Economy of Communism*. Princeton, NJ: Princeton University Press.
16. While the process of marketization is a necessary condition to economic modernization, it must be accompanied by *opening*. A more detailed discussion of these conditions can be found in Chap. 3.
17. Kornai, János. 1980. "The dilemmas of a socialist economy: the Hungarian experience." *Cambridge Journal of Economics* 4: 147–157; Kornai, János. 1992. *The Socialist System: The Political Economy of Communism*. Princeton, NJ: Princeton University Press.
18. Smith, Hazel. 2005. Hunger for Peace. Washington, DC: USIP; Woo-Cumings, Meredith. 2002. "The Political Ecology of Famine: The North Korean Catastrophe and Its Lessons." *Asia Development Bank. Research Paper Series* (31); Snyder, Scott & Flake, Gordon. 2003. *Paved with Good Intentions: The NGO Experience in North Korea*. Westport: Praeger.
19. Kornai, János. 1992. *The Socialist System: The Political Economy of Communism*. Princeton, NJ: Princeton University Press.
20. Kornai, János. 1992. *The Socialist System: The Political Economy of Communism*. Princeton, NJ: Princeton University Press.
21. Stradiotto, Gary & Guo, Sujian. 2007a. "Market Socialism in North Korea: A Comparative Perspective." *Journal of the Asia Pacific Economy* 12 (2): 188–214.
22. Stradiotto, Gary & Guo, Sujian. 2007a. "Market Socialism in North Korea: A Comparative Perspective." *Journal of the Asia Pacific Economy* 12 (2): 188–214 (citing Bardhan and Roemer, 1993, p. 3).
23. Stradiotto, Gary & Guo, Sujian. 2007a. "Market Socialism in North Korea: A Comparative Perspective." *Journal of the Asia Pacific Economy* 12 (2): 188–214.

24. Stradiotto, Gary & Guo, Sujian. 2007a. "Market Socialism in North Korea: A Comparative Perspective." *Journal of the Asia Pacific Economy* 12 (2): 188–214; Stradiotto, Gary & Guo, Sujian. 2007b. "The Nature and Direction of Economic Reform in North Korea." *Political Studies* 55: 754–778.
25. Stradiotto, Gary & Guo, Sujian. 2007a. "Market Socialism in North Korea: A Comparative Perspective." *Journal of the Asia Pacific Economy* 12 (2): 188–214; Stradiotto, Gary & Guo, Sujian. 2007b. "The Nature and Direction of Economic Reform in North Korea." *Political Studies* 55: 754–778 (citing Weisskopf, 1993, p. 122).
26. Stradiotto, Gary & Guo, Sujian. 2007a. "Market Socialism in North Korea: A Comparative Perspective." *Journal of the Asia Pacific Economy* 12 (2): 188–214.
27. Arnold, N. Scott. 1992. "Market socialism." *Critical Review* 6 (4): 517–557; Wan-wen Chu. 2010. "Market socialism, Chinese style: bringing development back into economic theory." *China Economic Journal* 3 (3): 307–312; Zheng, Ping & Scase, Richard. 2013. "The Restructuring of Market Socialism in China: an 'Agency' Perspective." *Thunderbird International Business Review* 55 (1).
28. Chu, Wan-wen. 2010. "Market Socialism, Chinese Style: Bringing Development Back Into Economic Theory." *China Economic Journal* 3 (3): 307–312.
29. Parts of the argument made by Chu (2010) go beyond the scope of this chapter, but they are worth mentioning. Since the 1978 reforms, institutional arrangements encouraged China's sustained growth through increases in aggregate supply rather than aggregate demand. China's market socialism resulted in the greater government intervention because of a larger gap between supply and demand, a greater need to socialize investment risks, and an imbalanced development process. Chu makes a convincing argument also for the advantages of Chinese market socialism, building on the argument made by Gerschenkron's argument that 'the development of a backward country may, by the very virtue of its backwardness, tend to differ fundamentally from that of an advanced country'. The speed and character of the industrial development can have some differences, because latecomers have to implement institutional instruments that have no counterparts in the industrialized countries. The degree of backwardness is also important. The latecomer does not possess enough capital, trained human resources, entrepreneurship and well-developed market institutions to start and sustain industrial growth. Gerschenkron argues that the more backward the latecomer, the bigger the tension between the current economic state and the great promise inherent in industrial development. In this view, if one assumes sufficient resources and removed bar-

riers to development, the potential of industrialization will depend on the degree of backwardness as well as the size of the backlog of technological innovations. Development will occur as a big spurt, not a gradual change. Overall, the bigger the gap between the backward and the advanced countries, the more inadequate the necessary supplies of capital, infrastructure and human resources in the latecomers. The Chinese government has largely intervened in socializing investment risks and promoting growth. The goal of economic development, and specifically a target rate of growth, was issued as a downward command from the central to the local government.

30. Everard, John. 2012. *Only Beautiful, Please: A British Diplomat in North Korea*. Baltimore: The Brooking Institution. pp. 94–95.
31. Hassing, Ralph & Oh, Kongdan. 2009. *Hidden People*. Maryland: Rowman & Littlefield Publishers. pp. 82–96.
32. Haggard, Stephan & Ryu, Jaesung. 2010. "Kim Jong Il on the Market: North Korea: Witness to Transformation blog." *Peterson Institute for International Economics*. Retrieved from http://www.piie.com/blogs/nk/?p=2495
33. Chung, Young Chul. 2004. "North Korean Reform And Opening: Dual Strategy and 'Silli (Practical) Socialism'." *Pacific Affairs* 71 (2): 283–304.
34. Chung, Young Chul. 2004. "North Korean Reform And Opening: Dual Strategy and 'Silli (Practical) Socialism'." *Pacific Affairs* 71 (2): 283–304.
35. Chung, Young Chul. 2004. "North Korean Reform And Opening: Dual Strategy and 'Silli (Practical) Socialism'." *Pacific Affairs* 71 (2): 283–304.
36. Cohen, Roberta. 2012. "Human Rights in North Korea: Addressing the Challenges." *International Journal of Korean Unification Studies* 22 (2): 29–62; Kim, Soo Am, Kim, Kook Shin, Kim, Young Yoon, Lim, Soon Hee, Jeong, Eun Mee & Park, Young Ja. 2012. *The Quality of Life of North Korean: Current Status and Understanding*. Seoul: KINU.
37. Fifield, Anna. 2019. *The Great Successor: The Secret Rise and Rule of Kim Jong Un*. New York: John Murray; Tudor, Daniel & Pearson, James. 2015. *North Korea Confidential*. Clarendon: Tuttle Publishing. p. 22; Smith, Hazel. 2015. *North Korea: Markets and Military Rule*. Cambridge: Cambridge University Press.
38. Smith, Hazel. 2000. "Bad, Mad, Sad or Rational Actor? Why the 'Securitization' Paradigm Makes for Poor Policy Analysis of North Korea." *International Affairs (Royal Institute of International Affairs 1944–)* 76 (3): 593–617; Smith, Hazel. 2005. *Hunger for Peace*. Washington DC: USIP; Snyder, Scott & Flake, Gordon. 2003. *Paved with Good Intentions: The NGO Experience in North Korea*. Westport: Praeger.
39. Eberstadt, Nicholas. 1999. *The End of North Korea*: 98–102. Washington, DC: The AEI Press.

40. Woo-Cumings, Meredith. 2002. "The Political Ecology of Famine: The North Korean Catastrophe and Its Lessons." *Asia Development Bank. Research Paper Series* (31): 24.
41. Ahn, Christine. 2005. Famine and the Future of Food Security in North Korea. *FoodFirst. Policy Brief* (11); Smith, Hazel. 2005. *Hunger for Peace.* Washington DC: USIP.
42. Smith, Hazel. 2005. *Hunger for Peace.* Washington DC: USIP; Howe, Brendan & Kim, Kah-ul. 2011. "North Korea: Policy Failures, Human Insecurity, Consequences, and Prescriptions." *Korea Observer* 42 (2): 281–310; Haggard, Stephan & Noland, Marcus. 2006. *The North Korean Refugee Crisis: Human Rights and International Response.* Washington, DC: U.S. Committee for Human Rights in North Korea; Haggard, Stephan & Noland, Marcus. 2011. "Gender in Transition: The Case of North Korea." *East-West Center, Economics Study Area* Series (124); Noland, Marcus. 2003. "Famine and Reform in North Korea." *Institute for International Economics*; Frank, Ruediger. 2005. "Economic Reforms in North Korea (1998–2004): Systemic Restrictions, Quantitative Analysis, Ideological Background." *Journal of the Asia Pacific Economy* 10 (3): 278–311.
43. In hindsight, it is worth asking whether a different set of choices and attitudes on part of the government could have mitigated the disastrous events of 1994–1998. The first step to answering this question is to understand the factors that contributed to the food shortages: an extractive planned economic system, the military-industrial complex prioritized over the agriculture sector, droughts, and the collapse of trade with the Soviet Union upon its dissolution in the 1990s. In 1945, socialism began with the state's seizure of all property and collectivization of the country. All farms and factories were nationalized in order for the state to control the means of production and then to redistribute food and goods among the population. With the state's seizure of control of the economy comes the state's responsibility to look after the needs of the people, though for a limited time, the regime chose, instead, to redirect funds generated by the agricultural sector to the development of heavy industry for industrialization. This prioritization is vividly illustrated in an article published in 1964 in the Labor Daily newspaper (Rodong Sinmun), 'Like our country which was predominantly a backward agricultural country, having achieved the socialist revolution, we succeeded in spurring the country's industrial growth in a limited time. The necessary funds must be secured from the agricultural sector'. See: Chan, Young Bang. 1995. *The Democratic People's Republic of Korea at a crossroad.* Seoul: Park Young-sa. pp. 99, 232–233. There are numerous statements from Supreme Leader Kim Il Sung that confide how North Korea had to pay such a high price to spur the indus-

trial growth for a strong national defense, for example, 'To achieve a rapid industrialization with the development of the military industrial complex, the state had to pay an enormous price' (Kim, Il Sung. 1983. *The collected works of Kim Il Sung[Kim Il Sung Jeojakjip]*. Pyungyang: Chosun Rodong Dang publishing company. p. 157) These direct sources demonstrate that Kim Il Sung didn't have any illusions about how the health and nutrition of the people were being exploited in order to build a strong military to defend the fatherland at all costs.

44. Yoon, In Ju. 2012. *The Privatization Phenomenon in North Korea [Bukhanui sayuhau hyonsang]*. Seoul: Korean Academic Information.
45. Fifield, Anna. 2019. *The Great Successor: The Secret Rise and Rule of Kim Jong Un*. New York: John Murray; Tudor, Daniel & Pearson, James. 2015. *North Korea Confidential*. Clarendon: Tuttle Publishing. p. 22; Lankov, Andrei. 2013. *The Real North Korea: Life and Politics in the Failed Stalinist Utopia*. Oxford: Oxford University Press. p. 131.Smith, Hazel. 2015. *North Korea: Markets and Military Rule*. Cambridge: Cambridge University Press.
46. Gorbachev (1987, p. 33) explained the essence of his reform as 'based on dramatically increased independence of enterprises and associations, their transition to full self-accounting and self-financing, and granting all appropriate rights to work collectives'. See: Gorbachev, Mikhail. 1987. *Perestroika: New Thinking for our Country and the World*. New York: Harper & Row. p. 33. As was witnessed in the former Soviet Union and East Germany, any such reform to improve efficiency from within the system is bound to fail, and North Korea was no exception.
47. Eberstadt, Nicholas. 2009. The North Korean Economy. London: Routledge. p. 78.
48. KEI Korea Economic Institute. 2018. North Korean Economic Forecast at http://keia.org/
49. Noland, Marcus. 2010. "North Korea's Failed Currency Reform." *Peterson Institute for International Economics*. Retrieved from https://www.piie.com/commentary/op-eds/north-koreas-failed-currency-reform
50. Yang, Moon-soo. 2014. *Economy and Society in the Kim Jong-un Era: New Relations Between the State and the Market [Kimjeongeunshidaeuigyeongjeawasahoe:gukgawasijangui saerowoon gwangye]*. Seoul: Hanul Academy. p. 228.
51. Mundy, Simon. 2014. "Elite splash out as Pyongyang keeps harsh reality away from prying eyes", *Financial Times*.
52. Lankov, Andrei. 2014. *The Real North Korea: Life and Politics in the Failed Stalinist Utopia*. Oxford: Oxford University Press. p. 131.
53. Lankov, Andrei. 2014. *The Real North Korea: Life and Politics in the Failed Stalinist Utopia*. Oxford: Oxford University Press. p. 131.

54. Ruwitch, John & Park, Ju-min. 2013. "Pyongyang losing grip on economy", *International New York Times.*
55. Ruwitch, John & Park, Ju-min. *op cit* 2013.
56. Ruwitch, John & Park, Ju-min. *op cit* 2013.
57. Tudor, Daniel & Pearson, James. 2015. *North Korea Confidential.* Clarendon: Tuttle Publishing. p. 22.
58. Tudor, Daniel & Pearson, James. 2015. *North Korea Confidential.* Clarendon: Tuttle Publishing. p. 22; Smith, Hazel. 2015. *North Korea: Markets and Military Rule.* Cambridge: Cambridge University Press.
59. It is worth specifying that in the new North Korean economy, there is no proper economic planning that comes from within the state. The reason for this is that there is no institutional support to normalize the economic cycle, no taxation system, no appropriate banking system. The consequence of this it is impossible to plan National because there are no real Investments made public social infrastructure worrying any infrastructure for production, also is no domestic currency that replaces domestic savings which means there is no capital accumulation for the National economy. The new class of *Donju* currently plays the role of banking the private sector. However, because there is no Central Bank, no budget can be allocated and no real efficient monetary system can be created. The current system of tolerated market activity and underground economy originated from the end of trade with the Communist Bloc in the 1990s which means this trade system currently operates without any real capital just as it receives no access to energy sources and no real means of production.
60. Jo, Seong Ju. 2014. "Marketisation and Gender in North Korea." In *Economy and Society in the Kim Jong Un Era [Kim Jong Un Shidaeui Gyungjaewa Sahoe]*, edited by Yang Mun Su. Seoul: Hanul. pp. 319–320.
61. Park, Kyung Ae. 1992. "Women and Revolution in North Korea." *Pacific Affairs* 65 (4): 527–545.
62. Woo-Cumings, Meredith. 2002. "The Political Ecology of Famine: The North Korean Catastrophe and Its Lessons." *Asia Development Bank. Research Paper Series* (31).
63. Lankov, Andrei, & Kim, Seok-hyang. 2008. "North Korean Market Vendors. The Rise of Grassroots Capitalists in A Post-stalinist Society." *Pacific Affairs* 81 (1): 53–72.
64. Yuzhe, Zhang and Ling, Wang. 2015. "Cheers, Fears for China's Next Step Overseas." *Financial Times.*
65. Food and Agriculture Organization of the United States/World Food Programme. 2019. "Democratic People's Republic Of Korea (DPRK)—FAO/WFP Joint Rapid Food Security Assessment. p. 22.

Bibliography

Ahn, Christine. 2005. "Famine and the Future of Food Security in North Korea." *FoodFirst. Policy Brief* (11).

Ahrens, Joachim. 2004. "Safeguarding Economic Cooperation, Reform, and Development on the Korean Peninsula." In *A Changing Korea in Regional and Global Contexts,* edited by Cho et al. Honolulu: University of Hawaii Press: 477–538.

Armstrong, Charles King. 2005. *The Two Koreas.* London: Routledge.

Armstrong, Charles King. 2009. "The Destruction and Reconstruction of North Korea, 1950–1960." *The Asia Pacific Journal* 7 (0): 1–9.

Arnold, N. Scott. 1992. "Market Socialism." *Critical Review* 6 (4): 517–557.

Chan, Young Bang. 1995. *The Democratic People's Republic of Korea at a Crossroad.* Seoul: Park Young-sa. pp. 99, 232–233.

Chu, Wan-wen. 2010. "Market Socialism, Chinese Style: Bringing Development Back into Economic Theory." *China Economic Journal* 3 (3): 307–312.

Chung, Young Chul. 2004. "North Korean Reform And Opening: Dual Strategy and 'Silli (Practical) Socialism'." *Pacific Affairs* 71 (2): 283–304.

Cohen, Roberta. 2012. "Human Rights in North Korea: Addressing the Challenges." *International Journal of Korean Unification Studies* 22 (2): 29–62.

Collins Business English Dictionary. n.d.-a Retrieved from https://www.collinsdictionary.com/dictionary/english/privatize.

Collins Business English Dictionary. n.d.-b Retrieved from https://www.collinsdictionary.com/dictionary/english/private-property.

Eaton, John. 1963. *Political Economy: A Marxist Textbook.* International Publishers. Reprinted 1970. p. 29.

Eberstadt, Nicholas. 1998. "North Korea's Interlocked Economic Crises: Some Indications from 'Mirror Statistics'." *Asian Survey* 38 (3): 203–230.

Eberstadt, Nicholas. 1999. *The End of North Korea.* Washington, DC: The AEI Press. pp. 98–102

Eberstadt, Nicholas. 2009. *The North Korean Economy.* London: Routledge. p. 78

Everard, John. 2012. *Only Beautiful, Please: A British Diplomat in North Korea.* Baltimore: The Brooking Institution. pp. 94–95.

Fifield, Anna. 2019. *The Great Successor: The Secret Rise and Rule of Kim Jong Un.* New York: John Murray.

Food and Agriculture Organization of the United States/World Food Programme. 2019. "Democratic People's Republic Of Korea (DPRK)—FAO/WFP Joint Rapid Food Security Assessment."

Frank, Ruediger. 2005. "Economic Reforms in North Korea (1998–2004): Systemic Restrictions, Quantitative Analysis, Ideological Background." *Journal of the Asia Pacific Economy* 10 (3): 278–311.

Fuller, Thomas. 2015. "Capitalist Soul Rises as Ho Chi Minh City Sheds Its Past." *The New York Times*. Retrieved from https://www.nytimes.com/2015/07/21/world/asia/ho-chi-minh-city-finds-its-soul-in-a-voracious-capitalism.html.

Gorbachev, Mikhail. 1987. *Perestroika: New Thinking for our Country and the World*. New York: Harper & Row.

Government of the DPRK. Constitution of the DPRK. 2014 edition.

Gray, Kevin & Lee, Jong-Woon. 2015. "Following in China's Footsteps? The Political Economy of North Korean Reform." *The Pacific Review* 30 (1): 51–73.

Haggard, Stephan & Noland, Marcus. 2006. *The North Korean Refugee Crisis: Human Rights and International Response*. Washington, DC: U.S. Committee for Human Rights in North Korea.

Haggard, Stephan & Noland, Marcus. 2011a. "Gender in Transition: The Case of North Korea." *East-West Center, Economics Study Area Series* (124).

Haggard, Stephan & Noland, Marcus. 2011b. *Witness to Transformation: Refugee Insights into North Korea*. Washington, DC: Peterson Institute for International Economics.

Haggard, Stephan & Ryu, Jaesung. 2010. "Kim Jong Il on the Market: North Korea: Witness to Transformation blog." *Peterson Institute for International Economics*. Retrieved from http://www.piie.com/blogs/nk/?p=2495.

Halliday, Jon. 1981. "The North Korean Model: Gaps and Questions." *World Development* 9 (9–10): 889–905.

Hassing, Ralph & Oh, Kongdan. 2009. *Hidden People*. Maryland: Rowman & Littlefield Publishers. pp. 82–96.

Hayek, Friedrich A. 1944. *The Road to Serfdom*. University of Chicago Press. pp. 91–92.

Hayek, Friedrich A. 1980. "The Uses of Knowledge in Society." In *Individualism and Economic Order*. Chicago: University of Chicago Press. p. 80.

Hee Soon, Lim. 2005. *The Food Crisis and the Changing Roles and Attitudes of North Korean Women*. KINU Studies Series 05-02. Seoul: Korean Institute for National Unification. Retrieved from http://repo.kinu.or.kr/bitstream/2015.oak/823/1/0000604095.pdf.

Howe, Brendan & Kim, Kah-ul. 2011. "North Korea: Policy Failures, Human Insecurity, Consequences, and Prescriptions." *Korea Observer* 42 (2): 281–310.

Jo, Seong Ju. 2014. "Marketisation and Gender in North Korea." In *Economy and Society in the Kim Jong Un Era [Kim Jong Un Shidaeui Gyungjaewa Sahoe]*, edited by Yang Mun Su. Seoul: Hanul.

KEI Korea Economic Institute. 2018. North Korean Economic Forecast at http://keia.org/

Killalea, Debra. 2016. "North Korea: Inside the lives of Pyongyang's rich kids." *News.com.au*. Retrieved from https://www.news.com.au/travel/travel-updates/travelstories/north-korea-inside-the-lives-of-pyongyangs-rich-kids/news-story/e9b4dae09f05dbc272495cce2dd9faee.

Kim, Byung-Yeon, Kim, Suk Jin, & Lee, Keun. 2007. "Assessing the Economic Performance of North Korea, 1954–1989: Estimates and Growth Accounting Analysis." *Journal of Comparative Economics* 35: 564–582.

Kim, Il Sung. 1983. *The collected works of Kim Il Sung [Kim Il Sung Jeojakjip]*. Pyungyang: Chosun Rodong Dang publishing company. p. 157.

Kim, Soo Am, Kim, Kook Shin, Kim, Young Yoon, Lim, Soon Hee, Jeong, Eun Mee & Park, Young Ja. 2012. *The Quality of Life of North Korean: Current Status and Understanding*. Seoul: KINU.

Kim, Sungwoo. 1993. "The Permanent Export Hypothesis and Foreign Trade of a Centrally Planned Economy: A Case Study of North Korea." *International Economic Journal* 7 (4): 49–57.

Kokko, Ari. 2005. "Economic Reforms and Skill Requirements in DPRK, European Institute of Japanese Studies" (unpublished policy paper, quotes with permission). Retrieved from http://vps.stanleyfoundation.org/initiatives/eenk/papers/Kokko.pdf.

Kornai, János. 1980. "The Dilemmas of a Socialist Economy: The Hungarian Experience." *Cambridge Journal of Economics* 4: 147–157.

Kornai, János. 1992. *The Socialist System: The Political Economy of Communism*. Princeton, NJ: Princeton University Press.

Lankov, Andrei, & Kim, Seok-hyang. 2008. "North Korean Market Vendors. The Rise of Grassroots Capitalists in A Post-stalinist Society." *Pacific Affairs* 81 (1): 53–72.

Lankov, Andrei. 2013. *The Real North Korea: Life and Politics in the Failed Stalinist Utopia*. Oxford: Oxford University Press. p. 131.

Lavoie, Don. 2016. *National Economic Planning: What Is Left?* Fairfax: George Mason University.

Li, Hung. 1977. *China's Political Situation and the Power Struggle in Peking*. Hong Kong: Lung Men Press.

Lim, Youngil. 2004. "The Technology Institutions-Productivity Nexus in the DPRK—A Comparative Perspective with the ROK." In *A Changing Korea in Regional and Global Contexts*, edited by Cho et al., 539–589. Honolulu: University of Hawaii Press. ISBN: 89-521-0565-6.

Metzger, Gillian E. 2003. "Privatization as Delegation." *Center for Constitutional Governance* 103 (1367): 1369.

MOU. 2019. "Weekly Report on North Korea." Retrieved from https://www.unikorea.go.kr/eng_unikorea/relations/infoNK/weekly/.

Noland, Marcus. 2003. "Famine and Reform in North Korea." *Institute for International Economics*.

Noland, Marcus. 2010. "North Korea's Failed Currency Reform." *Peterson Institute for International Economics*. Retrieved from https://www.piie.com/commentary/op-eds/north-koreas-failed-currency-reform

OECD. 2019. "GDP." Retrieved from https://data.oecd.org/korea.htm

Oishi, Takahisi. 2001. *The Unknown Marx: Reconstructing a Unified Perspective.* Foreword by Terrell Carver. London: Pluto Press.

Park, Kyung Ae. 1992. "Women and Revolution in North Korea." *Pacific Affairs* 65 (4): 527–545.

Park, Yong-Soo. 2009. "The Political Economy of Economic Reform in North Korea." *Australian Journal of International Affairs* 63 (4): 529–549.

Ruwitch, John. & Park, Ju-min. 2013. "Pyongyang Losing Grip on Economy." *International New York Times.*

Smith, Hazel. 1999. "'Opening Up' By Default: North Korea, the Humanitarian Community and the Crisis." *The Pacific Review* 12 (3).

Smith, Hazel. 2000. "Bad, Mad, Sad or Rational Actor? Why the 'Securitization' Paradigm Makes for Poor Policy Analysis of North Korea." *International Affairs (Royal Institute of International Affairs 1944-)* 76 (3): 593–617.

Smith, Hazel. 2005. *Hunger for Peace.* Washington, DC: USIP.

Smith, Hazel. 2015. *North Korea: Markets and Military Rule.* Cambridge: Cambridge University Press.

Snyder, Scott & Flake, Gordon. 2003. *Paved with Good Intentions: The NGO Experience in North Korea.* Westport: Praeger.

Stradiotto, Gary & Guo, Sujian. 2007a. "Market Socialism in North Korea: A Comparative Perspective." *Journal of the Asia Pacific Economy* 12 (2): 188–214.

Stradiotto, Gary & Guo, Sujian. 2007b. "The Nature and Direction of Economic Reform in North Korea." *Political Studies* 55: 754–778.

Tudor, Daniel & Pearson, James. 2015. *North Korea Confidential.* Clarendon: Tuttle Publishing. p. 22.

Von Mises, Ludwig. 1922. "Socialism: An Economic and Social Analysis." *Austrian School of Economics.*

Woo-Cumings, Meredith. 2002. "The Political Ecology of Famine: The North Korean Catastrophe and Its Lessons." *Asia Development Bank. Research Paper Series* (31).

Yang, Moon-soo. 2005. "North Korea's External Debts: Trend and Characteristics, Korea Focus." In *KDI Review of the North Korea Economy.* Seoul: Korea Development Institute.

Yang, Moon-soo. 2014. *Economy and Society in the Kim Jong Un Era: New Relations Between the State and the Market [Kimjeongeunshidaeuigyeongjeawasahoe: guk-gawasijangui saerowoon gwangye].* Seoul: Hanul Academy. p. 228.

Yoon, In Ju. 2012. *The Privatization Phenomenon in North Korea [Bukhanui sayu-hau hyonsang].* Seoul: Korean Academic Information.

Zheng, Ping & Scase, Richard. 2013. "The Restructuring of Market Socialism in China: An 'Agency' Perspective." *Thunderbird International Business Review* 55 (1). https://doi.org/10.1002/tie.21526.

CHAPTER 3

The Collapse Scenario: From Survival to Disintegration

1 Introduction

While Chap. 2 explores how and why the North Korean economy has reached an extreme state of distortion, as well as how sanctions have exacerbated the prevailing socioeconomic condition in the country, this chapter shifts to an examination of how the regime has managed to survive thus far. Whereas the previous chapter is a historical analysis which attempts to give a detailed background of the dysfunctional economy, this chapter offers a forecast of the two distinct paths the DPRK can now take—one in which Kim Jong Un seeks survival with nuclear weapons, thus instigating collapse, contrasted with one that assures survival and prosperity in exchange for denuclearization.

In this chapter, I analyze the six factors that have served to safeguard the regime's survival despite worsening conditions in North Korea and explain that, nevertheless, if the regime tries to survive with nuclear weapons, the likelihood of collapse is high. Some North Korean experts contend that, having lived through the catastrophic Arduous March of the 1990s, North Korea today will prevail in spite of hardship, but I must disagree. My projection is that the situation will differ drastically in the coming years and it will be much worse, based upon the following observations: critical GDP contraction, systemic food shortages, dollarization, corruption, hyperinflation, erosion of the regime's legitimacy coupled with the disintegration of internal and external control mechanisms, and

C. Y. Bang, *Transition beyond Denuclearisation*,
https://doi.org/10.1007/978-981-15-4316-6_3

mass defection, among other effects, will precipitate a region-wide geopolitical disaster, instigating the ultimate collapse of the regime, which will emanate humanitarian crisis.

Expounding upon clear logic as to why these factors are eroding, I analyze the reasons that the policy of denuclearization, which has been spearheaded by the U.S. and supported by the five stakeholder nations, has failed repeatedly to resolve the North Korean crisis. By explaining the fallacy of a "sticks alone" approach to negotiations with the DPRK, I demonstrate the necessity of a shared policy which coincide with the strategic interests of all of the stakeholder nations, not only the U.S., and which utilizes the respective "carrots" that each nation can offer.

What follows is a detailed explanation of the two disparate paths that the DPRK can follow out of the current impasse—one that leads to a "bright future" through rapid, sustained economic development and one that ends in calamity.

2 From Survival to Steady Erosion

2.1 *Why the Core Components that Served to Ensure the Regime's Survival Are Eroding*

How has North Korea been able to sustain the integrity and legitimacy of its regime thus far, in spite of acute social and economic hardship? In Chap. 2, I touched upon the five core elements that have helped North Korea to survive over the past several decades—idolization of the Supreme Leader under *Juche* ideology, nuclear weapons development, brutal punishment and repression, small coalition leadership and neglected bottom-up marketization.

However, the prevailing socioeconomic conditions in North Korea reveal that the factors that once helped the regime to survive are now quickly eroding, eventually instigating the ultimate collapse of the regime. Broadly, the following five factors (harsh economic sanction, contradictions between *Juche* ideology and reality, developing the nuclear weapons program, loss of internal and external control mechanisms, bottom-up dysfunctional marketization and the collapse of the small coalition leadership) can be attributed as major causes of the regime's quickly worsening survival chances.

2.2 Severe Contraction of North Korea's Gross National Product Due to Harsh Economic Sanctions

The progressively intensifying enforcement of sanctions by the international community have critically stunted economic activity. A considerable GDP contraction, –4.1%, was noted in 2018—the worst the nation has seen since 1997, while in the throes of the Arduous March. With exports for the same period decreased by 90% to a mere US $200 million, the enormous trade deficit (totaling approximately US $2.3 billion) will continue to be simply bankrolled by the state's foreign reserves, critically diminishing the state operational fund.

As the gap between the regime's revenue and expenditure widens, it will grow progressively worse, leading to an escalation in the extortion of overseas workers, the majority of whom live under poor conditions and retain meager cuts of their rightly-earned salaries. Likewise, exploitation of domestic labor will be precipitated as government officials squeeze workers in official sectors for bribes.

In the latter half of 2017, the North Korean regime lowered its daily rations quota from 400 grams of food per person to 300 grams, falling considerably short of its self-imposed goal of 573 grams per day, and measuring at exactly half of the United Nations' global nutritional standard of 600 grams per day. This substantial cut is indicative of the grim condition of the nation's agriculture systems, which for five consecutive years have come up nearly 500,000 metric tons short of the minimum output required to meet its self-imposed goal, according to figures supplied by the Rural Development Administration of South Korea. Ebbing trade with China will leave North Korea unable to supplement its waning supply with imported food.

This shortage will lead to inevitable famine and collapse of the central rationing system, as prolonged drought in the spring and summer of 2017 caused the loss of another 1.7% of the total harvest of rice, maize, and potatoes to be consumed in the 2018 crop year. In 2019, the food crop production is estimated to be the worst in 10 years, only 4.9 million metric tons.[1] Due to this sustained drought, approximately 10 million people now face imminent food shortages. Without a functioning rationing system, restrictions on mobility will weaken, and as food grows scarce, there will be a surge in unauthorized migration as millions of starving citizens seek sustenance. Just as the relative range of mobility increases, so will the unauthorized spread of information, uprooting the little remaining reverence the populace holds for Chairman Kim's regime as the reality of its dire situation becomes known to the population at large.

2.3 *Contradictions Between* Juche *Ideology and Reality*

The current crisis facing North Korea does not come from external threat, but stems from adherence to *Juche* ideology and the internal contradiction resulting from the sharp contrast between its promises of a "heaven on Earth" and the harsh reality on the ground.[2] Once ideological indoctrination begins to crumble along with the rationing system, the regime will resort to the only remaining bureaucratic control mechanism, namely criminal execution. Through the unified enforcement of ideological indoctrination, the rationing system and physical repression, the DPRK has succeeded in retaining the solidarity of the people.

The very unique *Juche* ideology and monolithic, dictatorial system of North Korea are the key elements that maintain the current regime and unite the North Korean people under harsh regimentation. The number of citizens brainwashed under this system of thought and the extent to which this idea solidifies the North's political system are detailed in the books of experts visiting or studying North Korea. In B.R. Myers' book, *The Cleanest Race*, the author describes North Koreans as "the cleanest race in the world" who literally believe in and accept everything of their leader with "pure hearts".[3] Of course, they have no comprehension that they have been brainwashed by ideology.

John Everard, who spent 900 days in North Korea as a British diplomat, looks at North Korea in this context.[4] Suki Kim, who visited North Korea as a journalist in 2002, tries to find the essence of the *Juche* ideology deeply embedded in North Korean society through meetings with the sons of the elite. In her book, *Without You, There Is No Us*, offers a moving and incalculably rare glimpse of life in the world's most unknowable country.[5] In the book, the author vividly conveys how North Korea's *Juche* is still "living" and moving the minds of the North Korean people. Another book entitled *Dear Leader* by Jang Jin-sung, tells the true story of a real North Korean defector and contains astonishing revelations about North Korea that could only be disclosed by an insider of the regime.[6] The book describes the author's escape, from a time when he was brainwashed by *Juche* to the moment he became aware of reality. For those who did not grow up in North Korea, it would be hard to imagine the shock of the author in that moment. Nevertheless, the common features of these books that explain the prevailing socioeconomic situation in North Korea carry a clear message—North Korea's *Juche* ideology is an important source of legitimacy for the survival of the North Korean regime.

2.4 Continuous Development of the Nuclear Weapons Program

The nuclear weapons development program has been an indispensable strategic asset to ensure the survival of the regime in North Korea.[7] Nuclear power is a means of credible deterrence against both real and imagined U.S. military threat.[8] We can take the former dictator of Libya, Muammar Gaddafi, as an example in understanding North Korea's ties to the nuclear weapons program. Gaddafi's fall from power and ultimate death in 2011 are understood by Kim Jong Un as being a direct consequence of his decommission of the nuclear weapons program in 2003.[9]

The development of nuclear weapons constitutes one of the two key pillars of the *byongjin* policy of North Korea, which enables sustaining the superiority of the military power over South Korea, which has a GDP 50 times larger than North Korea, at minimum cost, while simultaneously developing a nuclear powerhouse and pursuing economic modernization. Abandonment of nuclear development means abandonment of this dual line, *byongjin*.

With the great achievements of the governing regime that followed North Korea, Kim Il Sung, Kim Jong Il and Kim Jong Un, the nuclear weapons program has been used as a source of legitimacy.[10] The 2012 Constitution was enacted and reflected this major shift in its preamble: "Kim Jong-un has transformed our country into a strong military state, armed with nuclear weapons".[11]

In his first speech in 2012, Kim Jong Un repeatedly stated the paramount importance of raising living standards. A year later, he would make an even bolder claim. Having already had the constitution amended to declare the North a nuclear state, Kim Jong Un revived the *byongjin* policy of his grandfather. During a Workers' Party meeting in 1962, Kim Il Sung espoused a "simultaneous progress" policy that would pursue the development of the economy and national defense at the same time. "A gun in one hand and a hammer and a sickle in the other!" was Kim Il Sung's revolutionary slogan at the time. Fifty years later, Kim Jong Un again promoted the idea that this regime could pursue both nuclear weapons and economic development—that North Koreans could have both guns and butter.[12]

In addition to this, the nuclear weapons program has been used by the regime for decades to justify harsh labor extraction from the masses under the pretense of building credible military defense. Completion of the program's development in 2017 by Kim Jong Un marked a historic fulfillment of a path which the DPRK had diligently pursued since the 1980s, entailing the following main objectives: (1) credible domestic legitimacy to counterbalance the negative effects of an economy in decline; (2) supremacy over South Korea in defense capabilities; and (3) independent military deterrence without reliance on China or Russia.

However, the DPRK's nuclear weapons can no longer serve as either a negotiating tactic or a source of legitimacy, having lost the capacity to control through nuclear blackmail after making overtures towards the reconciliation of relations with the U.S. and South Korea in 2018–2019. Considering that Kim Jong Un has made a concerted effort since then to persuade world leaders, in particular Donald Trump, that he is ready to engage in negotiations, North Korea is subsequently unable to revert to a policy of nuclear blackmail.

2.5 *Loss of Control Mechanisms (Internal and External)*

2.5.1 *Erosion of Internal Control Mechanisms (1): Violent Repression and Social Control*

According to Kornai, the three essential components of the DPRK's internal bureaucratic control mechanism are (1) the rationing system, (2) ideological indoctrination and (3) punishment. With an already-distorted system which is now heavily aggravated by harsh economic sanctions, these fundamental mechanisms are beginning the break down, indicating an erosion of the regime's foundations. The regime will thus have to rely upon the only remaining internal control mechanism, harsh punishment.

Kim Jong Un's regime has already shown its propensity for physical punishment and large-scale executions, having ordered the deaths of nearly 400 individuals—a large segment of whom were senior party officials—since coming to power in 2011. Desperate to maintain absolute authority over its people, the state will commence a crusade of criminal prosecution against any who question the supremacy of the regime. The result will be a sharp upsurge in human rights violations, already exacerbated by the milking of remittances from overseas workers and income from domestic labor.

With human rights violations mounting and systems of bureaucratic control disintegrating, social unrest and widespread discontent will promptly follow, while rates of defection will climb sharply, already reaching 1127 in 2017 despite intense measures to consolidate security, especially along the Chinese-North Korean border. Once mobility accelerates due to unauthorized migration, information freely circulates, and the risk of staying behind outweighs that of defection, the massive outpour of North Korean defectors will prove to be a fatal blow to the deteriorating security of the regime.

Another important factor, however, is the *Inminban* system, a mechanism intended to exercise control over the family unit and neighborhood. To comprehend the scale of the *Inminban*, we can look to the activities of the East German secret police, the *Stasi*, for comparison. At the height of their espionage activity in the DDR, it was estimated that the ratio of informants to average citizens was somewhere between 1:6 and 1:7. In the *Inminban* system, this ratio is approximated at 1:3. The inference is that, in a nuclear family consisting of two parents and one child, one would almost certainly be keeping the others under surveillance.[13] The *Inminban*, however, is also gradually being put out of practice as a 2014 United Nations Commission of Inquiry investigation directed global attention to this human rights violation.

According to NKDB[14] "the situation of social control and repression has evolved as follows: The total number of cases: 46,713 (10.2% increase from the previous year) (of which 39,315 of witnessed or experienced cases, 84.2% / 7398 of informed cases and etc. 15.8%). Violation of Rights that have the highest occurrence rate: Right to Freedom and Individual Dignity (61.9%), Right to Liberty of Movement and Residence (12.6%) and Right to Life (10.6%) consist of 85.1% of total cases. Violation of Rights that have a medium occurrence rate: Right to Survival (3.3%), Rights Applicable to Arrested, Imprisoned, Detained, Accused or Convicted Persons (3.8%), Right to work (2.0%), Political Rights (1.4%) and Right to Health (1.1%).

The range of rates related to these rights is from 1 to 4. Violation of Rights that have a low occurrence rate: Each rate of Right to access to Education, Right to Marriage and Found a Family, Reproductive Right, Right to Religious Freedom and Expression, Right to Freedom of Assembly and Association, Right to property and Rights of Foreigners is below 1%. There was a consistent difference in the occurrence rates of each area of human rights violation between the 1990s to the 2000s, but since the year of 2010, the rates have been consistent."

2.5.2 Erosion of Internal Control Mechanisms (2): The Spread of Subversive Information About the Harsh Reality of Life

Over the decades, North Korea has historically blocked all exchanges of information with other nations, an important component in a control system aimed at preventing internal collapse, as discussed in greater detail in Sect. 3. With the advancements of technology and the spread of unofficial markets, however, they can no longer prevent the circulation of both incoming (anti-DPRK influence from abroad) and outgoing (insider knowledge of the failed socialist reality) unauthorized information. Through the dissemination of unauthorized information in the country, North Koreans have grown more cognizant of the reality of their situation, and once impenetrable ideological indoctrination has begun to erode.

To make a practical example: as previously discussed, the centralized North Korean rationing system has been crippled due to the collapse of the state manufacturing sector and the dismal crop harvest, a product of adverse weather conditions in recent years. A stark example of this was the 1.4 million metric ton grain shortage recorded in 2018. While the state previously allocated 573 grams of grain per capita, following recommended daily calorie intakes of 2000, after declines in food production, the central rationing system makes severe reductions. This fall in agricultural production, combined with declining imports of basic necessities, increasingly pushes North Koreans to greater mobility in search of food, more participation in the *Jangmadang* unauthorized markets and ultimate dissatisfaction with the regime and its ability to provide for the people. As the rationing system crumbles due to dismal agricultural production the reality of its dire situation becomes known to the population at large, rates of defection, currently estimated at more than 1000 annually, will continue to climb sharply. Once mobility expands and information freely circulates, the risk of staying behind will outweigh that of desertion, and defection will subsequently increase.

2.5.3 Erosion of External Controlling Mechanisms

Since its founding, North Korea has consistently employed hostile foreign policy. As Mikhail Gorbachev famously stated, foreign policy is an extension of domestic policy, which, in the case of North Korea, is a realization of *Juche* ideology, which is based upon hatred, the proletariat dictatorship, and class struggle. As an extension of its domestic policy, I can classify the North Korean regime's belligerency in dealings with the global community as yet another mechanism for control of the population and a method for ensuring its own survival. Built upon hatred and the socialist struggle against capitalism both inside and out, the regime has employed this hostile policy to coerce the sacrifice of the people to build credible military deterrence, as well as to justify the depravation of the people through the extraction system.

Communist systems are inherently hostile to outsiders who do not share their political ideology. This conflict is in itself a crucial component of communism, as it embodies the essential struggle against capitalism both inside and out. Eduard Shevardnadze, the Foreign Minister for the Soviet Union during President Gorbachev's term of office, had the following to say about the characteristics and essential nature of a radical totalitarianism socialist system:

> Renouncing the principle of the supremacy of universal human value and returning to the absolute of class origin means to resurrect the image of the enemy; internal or external and thus justifies repressions inside and outside the country. Presupposing a totally hostile encirclement means cultivating a siege mentality, preparing for war, and engaging in confrontations and conflict without respites.[15]

As the regime shifts towards reconciliation with the U.S. and South Korea and an emphasis on economic development, hostile foreign policy will be made obsolete. Moreover, were economic reform actually to be introduced to the DPRK, friendly foreign policy (and domestic policy along with it) would be necessitated. Unless hostility, hatred and animosity subside, Kim Jong Un will lose any chance of attracting investment or other funds from stakeholders and normal trade relationships can never be built with the outside. A more detailed discussion of this issue can be found in Chap. 4, under preconditions for reform of the system.

2.6 *Marketization from Below by Benign Oversight*

The regime's survival has long been dependent upon the leadership's acquiescence of the phenomenon of grassroots marketization, tolerated for several reasons: (1) it relieved the regime of responsibility to provide necessities; (2) it alleviated social and economic disaffection, especially stark deprivation during the Arduous March; and (3) it provided a chance for survival to millions of people during the harshest period between 1994 and 1999, delegating economic wellbeing to the population and, in practice, "allowing" them to engage in market activities. Now absolved of economic duty to the population, the regime was able to concentrate on fulfilling the *Seongun* (military first) policy.

According to the specialized website *DailyNK*, there are 387 officially-sanctioned markets within the country, with residents selling from over 600,000 stalls within these marketplaces.[16] According to this document, the protocols regarding general markets enacted in 2002 are listed in order of their relation to the size of urban areas[17]:

1. The Departments of commerce and the People's Committees in each province, county, and district or neighborhood responsible for the respective commercial industries shall establish one or more markets in an easily-accessible location, in accordance with each region's population size and unique regional characteristics, to be used by the municipal or town residences.

   The size of each market should depend on the population:
   - 600 stalls in a city or town of a population of 30,000–40,000
   - 900 stalls in a city or town of a population of 40,000–50,000
   - 1200 stalls in a city or town of a population of 50,000–70,000
   - 2000 stalls in a city or town of which the population size exceeds 70,000
2. Departments of commerce and the People's Committees in each province, and district and the respective commercial industries shall be allowed to designate titles of the markets according to the name of the specific municipality.
3. Departments of commerce and the People's Committees in each province, county, and district or neighborhood shall continue to modernize each market with renovations and/or expansions.
4. When building new markets, departments of commerce and the People's Committees in each province, county, and district or neighborhood shall consider local city planning designs, follow market design standards, and plan according to the finances of each town or city.

According to data from South Korea's Unification Ministry released in 1999, the transaction price of *Jangmadang* was 14 to 1667 times higher than the state price at the time. Thus, regulating *Jangmadang* appears to have been less effective due to the unique North Korean economic structure. Amid the food shortage, more than several hundred permanent *Jangmadang* were operating across North Korea, among them a large market with more than 10,000 people gathered. It is true that at that time, ordinary people were buying 60 percent of all staple grains and 70 percent of daily necessities from farmers' markets, so the second economy has been a very important part of the economy despite control.[18] On the impact of this expansion of the "second economy" on the political system, G. Gregory Grossman and G. Schopflin, argue that it enhances political stability because it meets the demands that the "first economy" does not meet.[19] Victor Nee and Peng Lian however, argues that a "second economy"—such as the one represented by the *Jangmadang in North Korea*—weakens the internal mechanism of the Party-state in the long term and causes cumulative change within the system.[20]

Indeed, the ripple effect of this "second economy" has shown a change in the relationship between the central and lower units through self-reliance imposed in North Korea. In North Korea, control over the party-state official and people has significantly weakened over time.[21] This expansion of the "second economy" is also directly affecting the formation of awareness among North Koreans. Based on the novels of Jeon Taek-cheol, Kang Hak-tae, and Ri Jeong-su, and the testimonies of North Korean defectors, the North Koreans seem to have common values such as individualism, compassion, and family values, which are considered secondary, although they are indoctrinated to retain the primary consciousness of self-reliance and collectivism and are submissive to the state monolithic supreme leadership.[22] However, according to testimonies from North Korean defectors and media organizations in South Korea and the West, core party members who direct and control residents are sitting on the sidelines about the residents' "secondary consciousness," and unless they grossly infringe upon state security, the state is almost giving up control.[23]

2.6.1 *Implications of Bottom-Up Marketization on Gender Hierarchies*

In North Korea, wealth and social status has traditionally been determined based on loyalty to the party and zeal for the revolution, which was based on the political background of the family. The problem is that there are gender-based differences in the process of determining this. The North's revolutionary-centered history, created with loyalty to the party and passion for the revolution, has been a history of men. Thus, the political hierarchy created on this basis was also hereditary through the male-dominated family, thus the male-centered hierarchy emerged.[24]

This distribution of capital on a political basis also affected activities in the market. Women were enabled to engage in market activities and gain some wealth but unable to ensure their own political protection. They had no choice but to rely on the existing political power structure, which is dominated by men, given that they had to secure political and economic power that would guarantee their safety even if they engaged in illegal business. In this way, the male-dominated hierarchy has been reenacted in the unofficial markets.

Gender hierarchies that are evident in society also are found in markets. State intervention in the market led to the establishment of a management system for the market.[25] The state began to directly coordinate market behavior of its residents through the market management office, thus delegating an enormous amount of power to coordinators who are typically male. A market manager directly managing a market has absolute power within a market, and a market manager is an entity exercising substantial power. The market manager is the general manager of the market and can exercise direct power to merchants because he has close ties to the interests of merchants in the market and is responsible for cracking down on irregularity and managing the market. People who do business in the market are mostly women, and managers are mostly male. Therefore, the male-dominated hierarchy is reenacted and men still exist as major actors of power in the market.[26]

2.7 *The Collapse of the System of Small Coalition Leadership*

As harsh economic sanctions take effect, GDP contracts sharply, the trade deficit grows and Kim Jong Un's foreign currency reserves dwindle, the future of the small coalition leadership system is unclear. Elite members of society who were previously rewarded generously with exclusive privilege and prize by the regime for their loyalty and support are now being deprived of their wealth and privilege as Kim Jong Un squeezes the *Donju* for resources in order to replenish depleted state operating funds.

According to a report published by the Korea Institute for National Unification in 1990, North Koreans were divided into the core class of 5.98 million (28 percent), the agitated class of 9.62 million (45 percent) and the antagonistic class of 5.77 million (27 percent) even before the current social deviance became serious.[27] This means the North Korean regime has failed to rapidly broaden its core class, from which it garners popular support for the regime. In addition, it is a dangerous sign that there are 5.77 million (27 percent) hostile groups due to unequal opportunities between Pyongyang citizens and local residents. This means that North Korea's more than 40 years of policies have only changed its class members, but have not succeeded in enhancing social unity and expanding the base of its supporters.[28]

The current governance of North Korea under Kim Jong Un represents, as mentioned in Chap. 2, the latest in a series of distortions of a traditional model of socialism, onto which several characteristics unique to North Korea have been grafted over time. North Korea shares with other socialist states an economic system which is fundamentally a totalitarian extractive system in nature,[29] serving the specific purpose of fostering a small number of elite that provide their support in exchange for special privilege. Elite coalitions are not a feature unique to the North Korean regime, but rather they are common to all totalitarian and authoritarian systems. They appear when the state cannot, in the long-term, maintain order, popular consensus or domestic legitimacy by sheer repression alone.[30] The findings of the scholarly literature on totalitarian systems, power coalitions and shared leadership have also been applied to the study of the North Korean regime in recent years.[31]

The intrinsic attributes of the contemporary leadership in North Korea has been identified by B. R Myers[32] and Patrick McEachern[33] as a small "elitist coalition" in which the leader chooses to share power and bestow economic opportunities upon a restricted group of local, clan or tribe leaders who, in turn, control segments of the army or population. This system can be understood as an extreme version of a Pareto distribution applied to political power, where by ensuring support from 10% of the population, the leader controls the remaining 90%.

The essential catalyst for this system is the creation and maintenance of an atmosphere of "permanent war footing" or "permanent militarization." The leadership must "preserve a mantle of revolution,"[34] a permanent state of war, to justify enormous sacrifices by the population. These sacrifices are imposed on the people to extract resources and are justified by keeping the country constantly militarized, so much so that North Korea has been defined as a "garrison state."[35]

By claiming a nearly "divine" mandate under *Juche* principles and drawing authority from the legacy of his grandfather and father, Kim Jong Un has managed to sustain his reign over the last eight years. In view of consolidating his reign, he has redirected all state funds—whether income from official economic activities or illegal trade—together with all labor and goods towards two goals: the first being the development of the nuclear program, which North Korea declared to be completed in 2017; and the second being the realization of showcase projects, mostly within Pyongyang.

These selected projects (usually in the construction industry) serve the purpose of (1) giving economic opportunities to elite members (both civil and military) and (2) showing the population that their sacrifices are not in vain but rather are essential to the building of a "strong and prosperous country [*gangseong daeguk*].

The problem with the extractive system and small coalition is that intense socioeconomic deprivation and sacrifices can be imposed on the population only for a limited period of time. Hardships can be justified by arguing that the country is enduring especially difficult times. This is what the "military-first" policy (*Seongun*) of Kim Jong Il was about, since it was established in 1995. As long as the regime can claim that there is an imminent threat, it can encourage individuals to accept extreme hardships with the promise of a better future.[36]

In the long run, however these calls to mass mobilization, food rationing, and heavy work schedules lose appeal and significance. The emergency becomes ordinary, and the promises of utopia are never realized.[37] At this point, the state must resort to other means to either coerce or motivate an increasingly skeptical and exhausted populace.

This system, perfected over his 7 years in power, has sustained Kim Jong Un well enough to allow him to complete the nuclear program and to initiate a course of negotiations with other world leaders (Trump, Xi, Moon, and Putin). However, due to the unbearable economic pressure coming from international sanctions, the small coalition system is now in jeopardy.[38]

3 The Endgame That Can Never Be Won

For North Korea, negotiations for denuclearization are an endgame scenario: with or without nuclear weapons, the DPRK must seek survival. From the U.S. vantage point, a nuclear-armed North Korea is no more than a regional threat, but for the remaining stakeholder nations, the stakes are much higher. The collateral damage resulting from armed conflict with the DPRK would be devastating and have tremendous political, economic, and humanitarian cost for neighboring countries. As the pressure of the "sticks" applied by the international community grows unbearable, Kim Jong Un may resort to extreme measures, unless a tangible plan for denuclearization is put forward—one which takes into account the true nature of the nuclear weapons program and offers a viable alternative for survival.

3.1 *The Arsenal of Sticks*

There is an array of methods of pressure exertion which can be exercised by the U.S. and other stakeholders, both collectively and individually, including but not limited to joint military exercises, censure for human rights violations, diplomatic isolation, secondary boycotts, inspections on international waters, blacklisting and punitive measures (punishment). These measures are active in nature, but passive threats are exerted, as well, such as the "temporary" closing of the Kaesong Industrial Complex.

On the side of the DPRK, only one weapon is available—testing of nuclear weapons and long-range missile systems. These threats, however, are intangible and do not inflict any real damage upon the U.S., South Korea, or any other perceived enemy. The "sticks" that the five stakeholder nations have applied in attempts to coerce North Korea, though, are very tangible, and their effective use can deal a serious blow to the regime. One form of punishment is exceptionally lethal—internationally- and unilaterally-imposed economic sanctions.

The UNSC's 2017 escalation of bans on North Korea's coal, mineral, textile, and seafood exports cut annual export revenue by more than $2 billion in 2018. Energy products, including coal and minerals, together with textiles have composed the nation's top two exports since 2011, and they alone accounted for a loss of more than $1.7 billion upon implementation of the UNSC resolutions 2371 and 2375.

The unilateral sanctions imposed on the DPRK by the U.S. restrict far more economic activities and target a much broader list of individuals and businesses than the sanctions issued multilaterally by the United Nations Security Council.[39] They are primarily designed to impede Pyongyang's development of missile and nuclear technology, but some have come in response to North Korean cyber-attacks—such as its 2014 breach of

Sony's computer systems—human rights violations; censorship; and money laundering, among other activities. Additionally, the U.S. has sanctioned banks, companies, and individuals outside North Korea, particularly in China and Russia, for supporting its weapons program. It has also fined companies for violating U.S. export controls. Additionally, in 2017, the U.S. Congress passed a piece of legislation, the Countering America's Adversaries Through Sanctions Act, which imposes further sanctions on North Korea (as well as on Iran and Russia), prohibiting certain types of U.S. assistance to foreign governments that aid North Korea.[40]

Some South Korean leaders have maintained a hard line against North Korea, while others, including the current president, Moon Jae-in, have opted for a more conciliatory approach, attempting to expand bilateral exchanges as a path toward peaceful coexistence. Seoul provided Pyongyang $7 billion in aid between 1991 and 2015,[41] usually in the form of food and medical assistance. In 2019, South Korea pledged another $8 million in aid and fifty thousand tons of rice—its first donation since 2015—to alleviate severe food shortages.[42] Some experts argue that these policies have diluted the effects of sanctions.

Tokyo has also restricted commercial and diplomatic exchanges with North Korea, imposing sanctions starting in 2006. In 2014, however, some were lifted to induce Pyongyang to investigate the disappearances of Japanese nationals in the 1970s and 1980s. In response to nuclear missile tests, Japan imposed new sanctions in February 2016, and again in August and December 2017. The sanctions were extended by two years in 2019, a few days before they were set to expire. These measures freeze certain North Korean and Chinese assets, ban bilateral trade with North Korea, restrict the entry of North Korean citizens and ships into Japanese territory, and prohibit remittances worth more than $880. North Korea has refused to cooperate in the probe regarding the abducted Japanese nationals until these sanctions are lifted. Japan has also played a sanctions monitoring role, tracking North Korean cargo transfers in regional waters.

In the past, North Korea's saving grace has been China's reluctance to crack down on unauthorized trade, but China has shown willingness in recent years to faithfully abide by its commitment to UNSC sanctions,[43] reducing imports from North Korea by 86.1% at the beginning of 2018, and likewise cutting their imports from the nation by 34%.

3.2 *The Consequences of Sanctions Enforcement*

Should the current sanctions-only strategy persist as the prevailing approach to the denuclearization of North Korea, the aftermath of the ensuing economic crisis, humanitarian disaster, and regime collapse would be incalculably costly. Below, I summarize some of the most tangible consequences of the exertion of economic pressure against the DPRK.

3.2.1 *Negative Economic Growth*

The progressively intensifying enforcement of sanctions by the international community have critically stunted economic activity. A considerable GDP decline, 4.1%, was noted in 2018—the worst the nation has seen since 1997, while in the throes of the Arduous March. With exports for the same period decreased by 90% to a mere US $200 million, the enormous trade deficit (totaling approximately US $2.3 billion) will continue to be simply bankrolled by the state's foreign reserves, critically diminishing the state operational fund.

3.2.2 *Dollarization*

Financing massive administration costs, the state has been forced to prop up the North Korean economy with foreign currencies such as the U.S. dollar, Chinese yuan, and euro. In *Jangmadang* as well, the overwhelming majority of trade is conducted in foreign currencies. As the won steadily declines and hyperinflation ensues, foreign currency has continued to dominate trade activity, creating stark income disparity between state workers and those employed by the unofficial sector.

3.2.3 *Overreliance on China*

In 2014, North Korea's dealings with China grew to account for over 90% of its total trade. The state relies upon imports of China to provide the most basic of necessities, commodities like crude oil, as well as televisions, mobile phones, and automobiles. Meanwhile, exports to China, the only market to which any North Korean goods are exported, are largely composed of low-value-added goods like coal, iron, and textiles. This overwhelming trade deficit reveals a perilous dependency on China, devaluing North Korean goods dramatically and leaving the economy highly vulnerable to the effects of internationally-imposed sanctions.

3.2.4 *Disintegration of the manufacturing sector*

Suffering from a chronic lack of electricity and raw goods and resources restricted by international sanctions, the state's manufacturing sector has all but crumbled. Industrial facilities across the country are in shambles, and the absence of necessary materials and modern technology have further stunted manufacturing activity. Reflecting the absurdity of the disfigured centralized economy, factory workers, earning meager salaries, pay into systems of bribery in order to miss work "unnoticed" and, instead, participate in the unofficial markets, where the return on their time and labor is exponentially more lucrative.

3.2.5 *Food shortage*

A 10% downturn in economic production and the worst drought to strike the nation in decades have led to food shortages of incredible proportions. An estimated 1.4 million ton grain shortage in 2018 has left North Korea even more reliant on imports, though ebbing trade with China will leave the state ultimately unable to supplement its food store, as in recent years, with hundreds of thousands of tons of imported food goods—leaving 25 million North Koreans critically malnourished. In 2019, the World Food Program (WFP) described under-nutrition in the country as "chronic and widespread," and noted that "many rural areas continue to face a nutrition crisis and require urgent and sustained support."[44]

3.2.6 *Extractive nature of the system*

As the economy grows further distorted and state operational funds deplete, the system becomes progressively more exploitative in nature. From its inception, the North Korean economy was intended to be *extractive* rather than *redistributive*, but the ever-widening gap between the regime's revenue and expenditure has left the regime desperate, leading to an increase in the extortion of overseas workers, the majority of whom live under poor conditions and remit all but meager portions of their earned salaries. Likewise, exploitation of domestic labor, as well as rampant bribery and other forms of corruption will continue to expand as government officials squeeze the civilian sector for income.

3.2.7 *Increase in defection*

With human rights violations and labor exploitation mounting and systems of centralized control disintegrating, social unrest and widespread discontent will promptly follow. As the reality of its dire situation becomes known to the population at large, rates of defection, currently estimated at more than 1000 annually,[45] will climb sharply. Once mobility expands, information freely circulates, and the risk of staying behind outweighs that of defection, the massive outpour of North Korean defectors will be a fatal blow to the deteriorating regime. Recent instances of defection of high-ranking secret police officials confirm this reality (Fig. 3.1).

3.3 The Nature of the Nuclear Weapons Program

As the stakes grow higher with the ever-increasing intensity of economic sanctions, the regime exerts their limited resources to expand testing of nuclear weapons and long-range missile systems, the only form of threat that they are able to apply. The possibility cannot be ruled out that Kim Jong Un may employ military provocation to induce coercive negotiations with the U.S. if the scope of sanctions and pressure against the DPRK continue to escalate. Since the collapse of working-level negotiations between the U.S. and North Korea, which resumed in Sweden on Oct. 5, 2019, the North's state media has continued to insist on self-reinforcement, with the possibility of carrying out large-scale provocations, including intercontinental ballistic missiles, to bolster the North's negotiating power.[46]

However, to understand North Korea's inability to emerge as the victor of this endgame scenario, one must comprehend the true nature of the nuclear weapons program. All weapons of mass destruction in possession of the regime are purely defensive in scope—they can never be applied to achieve the strategic objectives of conquering South Korea or attacking the U.S, nor can they be sold or traded for any kind of monetary gain. They are exclusively a measure of deterrence; North Korean long-range missiles may have the capacity to strike San Francisco, but employing them to such an end would be unthinkable.

3.4 No One on North Korea's Side

The game, therefore, can never be won by North Korea or any other actor, and the stakeholders are cognizant of this, even the DPRK's staunchest allies, China and Russia. Each of the members of the Six-party Talks have their own contrasting concerns and strategic interests, but all five adamantly oppose the establishment of North Korea as a nuclear power. Why is this so?

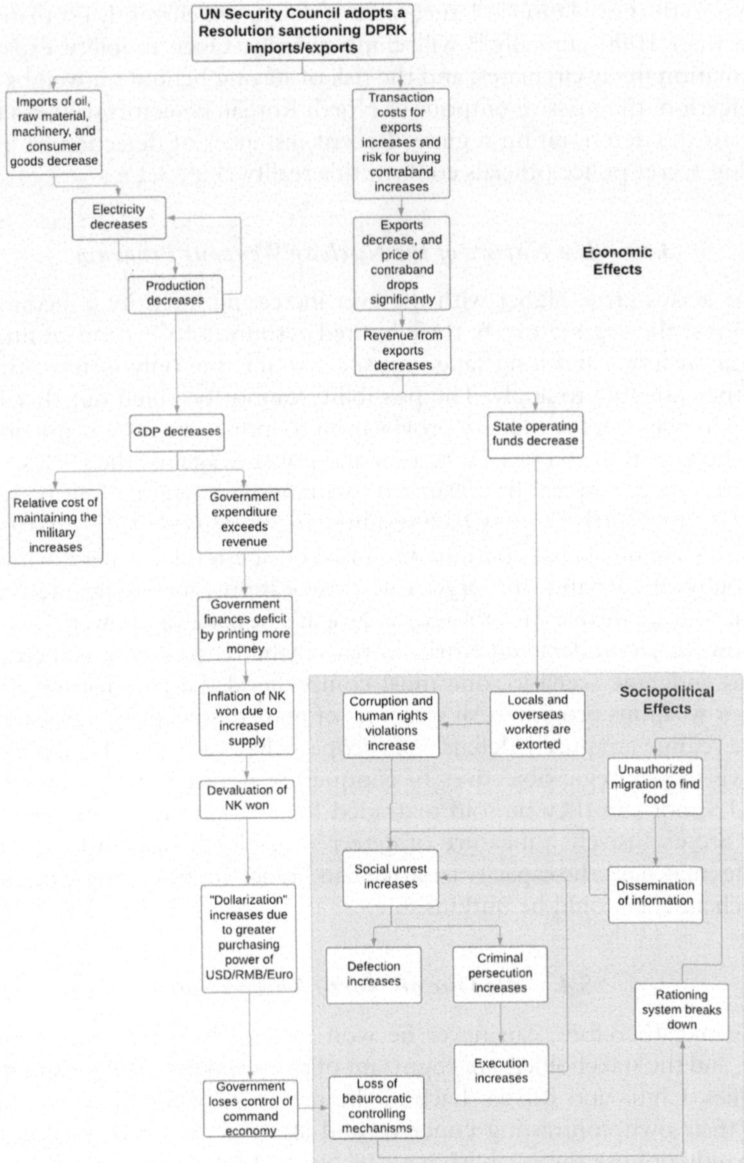

Fig. 3.1 Demonstrates the combined economic and sociopolitical effects that will destabilize and threaten the survival of the regime

Though China has asserted itself as the DPRK's final lifeline to trade and economic aid, a fundamental mistrust exists between the nations. North Korea views its powerful neighbor as having abandoned the essential tenets of socialism through their embracing of economic modernization and transformation to a market-oriented system, not to mention their perceived betrayal through compliance with UNSC sanctions, led by the U.S. Moreover, the very nature of the DPRK is one that mistrusts outsiders and maintains a military footing at all times.

Additionally, China and Russia view North Korea's achieving the status of a nuclear state as plausible justification for other neighboring countries, like South Korea and Japan, to rearm with nuclear capabilities. This geopolitical arrangement goes against the authoritarian states' interests, especially if the U.S. were to take advantage of such a climate to deploy high-tech weapons to the Korean Peninsula. Any expansion of U.S. influence or military power in the region is a fundamental threat to the security of China and Russia.

In this endgame scenario, even North Korea's allies will abandon them in the case of a nuclear standoff, but, even so, if threat continues to be the stakeholders' only approach to persuading Kim Jong Un to disarm, he will never accept without recourse through a viable exit strategy for survival. Instead, he will resort to armed confrontation, which will ultimately precipitate the collapse of the regime, a bloody resolution to the nuclear crisis that will instigate geopolitical and humanitarian disaster. Therefore, to achieve peaceful denuclearization and transform North Korea into an economically prosperous country, heavy pressure from the collective stakeholders must be combined with promise of reward. In other words, the "stick" must be dependent upon the "carrot"—Kim Jong Un must be convinced that regime survival is impossible without accepting denuclearization, while the reward for denuclearization must be so great that it renders the nuclear weapons program obsolete.

4 The Necessity of "Carrots" and the Rationality of Kim Jong Un

4.1 Kim Jong Un's Cost-Benefit Calculation

In considering the likelihood that Kim Jong Un will accept denuclearization in exchange for spectacular reward, I examine the Supreme Leader's demonstrated sound insight and judgment capabilities, demonstrated since coming to power in 2012 after the death of his father, Kim Jong Il.

In journalist Anna Fifield's *The Great Successor*, she characterizes Kim Jong Un as a "rational actor" whose single goal in life is to hold on to power. His development of the nuclear weapons program as a tool for coercive diplomacy and his ability to negotiate with world leaders, particularly in the U.S., has exemplified the stark contrast between him and his father and grandfather. By setting a new path for the nation towards economic development, we can see that he is capable of assessing the situation of the regime and making calculated decisions.

In order to follow through on the promises of a "bright future" and the establishment of the DPRK as a true "heaven on Earth," Kim Jong Un, making a calculation of cost versus benefit, should opt to give up nuclear weapons and ensure system survival through economic development under the guarantee of security and economic development funds to be provided by the five-member countries.

If we move forward with the premise that Kim Jong Un will choose a policy of economic opening and reform as a trade-off for denuclearization through reasonable calculations as a highly capable leader, what is the most effective path to modernization beyond denuclearization and mere survival? What blueprint can all five stakeholder countries, including North Korea, support in order to prosper, avoiding collapse of the regime and regional disaster?

4.2 *Addressing the True Nature of the Nuclear Weapons Program*

North Korean experts who have studied and watched North Korea since the collapse of the North American summit between Kim Jong Un and President Trump in Hanoi in February 2019 have expressed their views that Kim Jong-un has no intention of giving up his nuclear weapons development program. Among them are former DPRK Ambassador to the UK turned South Korean lawmaker, Tae Yong Ho,[47] and Professor Andrei Lankov of Kookmin University.[48]

Notably, as previously mentioned, the former U.S. Director of National Intelligence, Dan Coates, stated that "North Korea will seek to retain its WMD capabilities and is unlikely to completely give up its nuclear weapons and production capabilities because its leaders ultimately view nuclear weapons as critical to regime survival."[49]

However, through analysis of the true nature of the nuclear weapons program and the rationality of Chairman Kim Jong Un, I have come to the conclusion that it is highly likely that the regime will accept denuclearization if a viable, effective policy recommendation is presented. However, any proposal must entail both sticks and carrots from all five of the stakeholder nations, and it must account for the core functions performed by nuclear weapons.

To the Kim Jong Un regime, nuclear weapons serve a four-fold purpose as:

1. A deterrence measure against both real and perceived threat;
2. A source of domestic legitimacy and fulfillment of inherited legacy;
3. Cost-effective means of maintaining balance in military power with South Korea; and
4. A stabilizing factor against external threat.

Unless the reward offered to Kim Jong Un provides viable alternatives to each of these four elements, it will never stand a chance at inducing denuclearization.

4.3 Replacing the Current Safeguards of the Nuclear Weapons Program

In order to convince North Korea to accept denuclearization and transform into an economically prosperous, normalized state, any policy put forth must entail the following benefits (to be discussed in greater detail in Chap. 4):

1. *Military/political*

   All threat of military or political pressure must be withdrawn through the implementation of a variety of measures. Security guarantees from the U.S. and South Korea must be issued, accompanied by an end to joint military exercises and the U.S.' ultimate withdrawal from the Korean Peninsula. Diplomatic relations between North Korea and each of the stakeholders must be established, and all internationally- and unilaterally-imposed sanctions must be lifted. Peace treaties between the DPRK and the U.S. and South Korea must be instituted, with guarantees from the South that it will honor a future "one country, two systems" framework, while alliances with China and Russia should be reassured.

2. *Economic*

   Providing Kim Jong Un with a new source of domestic legitimacy, means of continuing his dynastic legacy and maintaining the power balance with South Korea will demand rapid economic growth—an annual GDP increase of at least 10% over a period of 10 years. Such spectacular development will require significant funds, a total of $300 billion over the same period, according to my calculations, be provided by South Korea, in addition to wartime reparations from Japan. Additionally, each of the stakeholder nations should provide their support in North Korea's membership in the IMF and World Bank in order to secure additional development funds. These economic resources are necessary to ignite growth, keep the elite happy, reallocate all low-level military personnel into the labor market and build infrastructure and institutions.

5 Conclusion

In this chapter, I presented compelling evidence that the core elements that have sustained the North Korean thus far are in a state of disintegration, and that the loss of internal and external controlling mechanisms is a foreboding omen for the future of Kim Jong Un and the country overall. The state of extreme breakdown indicated by the phenomena described—contracted GDP growth, dollarization and inflation, the waning loyalty of the small coalition leadership, overreliance on China, human rights violations, breakdown of the rationing system, the growing extractive nature of the system, and increases in defection—means that only violence and fear remain as a mechanism for control of the population.

Until recent years, the Kim dynasty's pursuit of nuclear capabilities as a means of survival has served them well. The nuclear policy has for years consolidated the legitimacy of the supreme leader by demonstrating self-sufficiency and military might while safeguarding *Juche* ideology, and it has galvanized support from the top military and communist party leadership.

Now, however, in depth analysis reveals that the nature of the geopolitical game is asymmetrical, and that North Korea's tactical strategy of nuclear brinkmanship is an endgame scenario which the regime has no chance of winning. While Kim Jong Un's bellicose threats contain only intangible and insubstantial harm, as inciting a nuclear war would unequivocally obliterate the DPRK, the five stakeholders' rebukes inflict real damage to the regime. Economic sanctions, the most lethal pressure exerted by the international community, have rapidly exacerbate North Korea's economic decline, accelerating the disintegration of the foundations of the regime.

Through examination of the last 25 years of attempted denuclearization policies and the constraints on the DPRK, it becomes clear that taking a "sticks alone" approach to coercing the regime to give up their nuclear weapons is untenable at the very least. Even though economic sanctions are strangulating the North Korean economy, compelling further concessions from the regime is a forgone conclusion. This should come as a grave warning to the five stakeholders, as, if North Korea is backed further into this impasse, they will be faced with two options: armed provocation or the collapse of the regime. As can surmised from past behavior, the leadership will not willfully accept the latter scenario.

Thus, North Korea now stands at a crossroads. After critical investigation, I have come to the conclusion that the only viable path to survival and the establishment of permanent peace and prosperity is through the abandonment of the nuclear weapons program in exchange for rapid economic modernization. Should Kim Jong Un make a rational calculation of the costs and benefits, thus accepting denuclearization, he can change the nature of the geopolitical game and build a winning exit strategy with survival through economic prosperity and permanent peace. The regime must recognize that survival of the regime will demand that they broker a deal to exchange nuclear weapons for security guarantees and a development fund to carry out the economic modernization drive and transition to market socialism. Time is not on North Korea's side. The dire circumstances of the contemporary DPRK demand that Kim Jong Un make the bold and audacious decision to blaze a new trail towards a "bright future."

Notes

1. https://www.wfp.org/news/after-worst-harvest-ten-years-10-million-people-dprk-face-imminent-food-shortages.
2. Joong-Ang Ilbo reports. 2017. "Korea's economic assistance should be reformed and opened by the U.S. government." [Hangukgyungjeajiwon, michejeabojangeurobukgyehteokgaebanghaeya]. Retrieved from https://news.joins.com/article/22074358.
3. Myers, Brian Reynolds. 2010. *The Cleanest Race: How North Koreans See themselves and why it matters*. New York: Melville House.
4. Everard, John. 2012. *Only Beautiful, Please: A British Diplomat in North Korea*. Baltimore: The Brooking Institution.

5. Kim, Suki. 2014. *Without you, there is no us: my time with the sons of North Korea's elites.* New York: Crown Publishers.
6. Jang, Jin-sung. 2014. *Dear Leader.* London: Ebury Publishing.
7. Stricker, Andrea & Albright, David. 2019. "How North Korea can be convinced to give up nuclear weapons." *NK News.* Retrieved from https://www.nknews.org/2019/01/how-north-korea-can-be-convinced-to-give-up-nuclear-weapons/.
8. Martin, Bradley K. 2019. "How the US president could earn his Nobel". *Asia Times.* Retrieved from https://www.asiatimes.com/2019/06/article/how-the-us-president-could-earn-his-nobel/.
9. Battacharjee, Anjali & Salama, Sammy. 2003. Libya and Nonproliferation. *Center for Nonproliferation Studies*; Braut-Hegghammer, Malfrid. 2009. "Libya's Nuclear Intentions: Ambition and Ambivalence." *Center Contemporary Conflict.* Retrieved from http://www.nps.edu/Academics/centers/ccc/publications/OnlineJournal/2009/Apr/braut-hegghammer-Apr09.pdf; Squassoni, Sharon & Feickert, Andrew. 2004. *Disarming Libya: Weapons of Mass Destruction.* Washington, DC: CRS Report for Congress; US Congress. 1996. Iran and Libya Sanctions Act of 1996. Retrieved from http://www.fas.org/irp/congress/1996_cr/h960618b.htm.
10. Bang, Chan Young. 1995. *The Democratic People's Republic of Korea at a crossroad*, Park Young-sa. pp. 99, 232–233.
11. Yonhap. 2019. "N. Korea changes constitution to make Kim Jong-un official head of state." *The Korea Herald.* Retrieved from http://www.koreaherald.com/view.php?ud=20190711000731.
12. Fifield, Anna. 2019. *The Great Successor: The Divinely Perfect Destiny of Brilliant Comrade Kim Jong Un.* New York: Public Affairs. p. 104.
13. KINU. 2007. *White Paper on human Rights in North Korea.* Seoul: Centre for North Korean human Rights Studies.
14. NKBD Database Center for North Korean Human Rights. Findings. Retrieved from http://www.nkdb.org/en/database/findings.php.
15. Shevardnadze, Eduard. 1991. *The Future Belongs to Freedom.* New York: The Free Press. pp. 57–58.
16. DailyNK. 2018. "Report: The Creation of the North Korean Market System." Retrieved from https://www.dailynk.com/english/notices/?mod=document&uid=68.
17. Cha, Victor & Collins, Lisa. 2018. "The Markets: Private Economy and Capitalism in North Korea?" *Beyond Parallel.* Retrieved from https://beyondparallel.csis.org/markets-private-economy-capitalism-north-korea/. The CSIS websites cites an official document issued by the DPRK government to confirm and explain the setting up and 'unofficial' regulation of markets: namely the "Korea's Commercial Order of the Democratic People's Republic of Korea," No. 48, May 20, 2003. Pyongyang.

"Commercial Holy Place of the Democratic People's Republic of Korea," [Joshunminjujuui inmingonghwaguk sangeopjishi]. No. 48, May 20, 2003). The document is Pyongyang, "Korea's Commercial Order of the Democratic People's Republic of Korea," No. 48, May 20, 2003. 평양, "조선민주주의 상업성지시," 제48호, 2003년 5월 20일 as quoted in https://beyondparallel.csis.org/markets-private-economy-capitalism-north-korea/.

18. Dong, Yong-seung. 1997. "The Impact of the Black Market Spread on the North Korean Economy." [Amsijang hwaksani bukhangyeongjeaae mich-ineun yeonghyang]. *Monthly Samsung Economic Group.*
19. Grossman, Gregory. 1977. "The 'Second Economy' of USSR." *Problems of Communism* 26 (5); Schophlin, George. 1993. *Politics in Eastern Europe, 1945–1992.* Oxford: Blackwell Publishers.
20. Nee, Victor & Lian, Peng. 1994. "Sleeping with the enemy: why communications love the market." *Theory and Society* 23 (2).
21. Jeong, Se-jin. 2000. *From Plan to Market: Political Economy of the North Korean regime [Gyehuyeseo sijanguro: Bukhan chejebyendong jeongchi kyungje yengu].* Seoul: Hanul Academy. pp. 20–32.
22. Huh, Man-ho. 2008. *Reform of North Korea: Openness and Human Rights [Bukhanui gaehyeokgaebanggwainkwon].* Seoul: Master Culture History. p. 36.
23. Huh, Man-ho. 2008. *Reform of North Korea: Openness and Human Rights [Bukhanui gaehyeokgaebanggwainkwon].* Seoul: Master Culture History. p. 36.
24. Park, Soon-sung and others. 2009. "North Korean defectors in the process of defection and resettlement." [Talbuk yeosunguitalbukmit jungchak gwajeongaeseouiinkwonchimhaesiltaejosha]. *National Human Rights Commission of Korea.* p. 53.
25. [21] Yang, Moon-soo. 2014. *Economy and Society in the Kim Jong-un Era: New Relations Between the State and the Market [Kimjeongeunshidaeuigy-eongjeawasahoe: gukgawasijangui saerowoon gwangye].* "Chapter 10. Marketization and Gender of North Korea." Seoul: Hanul Academy. p. 302.
26. Yang, Moon-soo. 2014. *Economy and society in the Kim Jong-un era: New relations between the state and the market [Kimjeongeunshidaeuigyeongjeawasahoe: gukgawasijangui saerowoon gwangye].* "Chapter 10, Marketization and Gender of North Korea." Seoul: Hanul Academy. p. 303.
27. Tongilwon, 1990. *North Korean dog '91' [Bukhangaeyo].* Seoul: Tongilwon. p. 238.
28. Huh, Man-ho. 2008. *Reform of North Korea. Openness and Human Rights [Bukhanui gaehyeokgaebanggwainkwon].* Seoul: Master Culture History. p. 39.

29. Jones-Rooy, Andrea & Prusher, Ilene. 2018. "Even Dictators Like Kim Jong Un Need To Keep Some People Happy." *FiveThirtyEight*. Retrieved from https://fivethirtyeight.com/features/even-dictators-like-kim-jong-un-need-to-keep-some-people-happy/; Chotiner, Isaac. 2019. "The early life of Kim Jong Un." *The New Yorker*. Retrieved from https://www.newyorker.com/news/q-and-a/the-early-life-of-kim-jong-un; Huang, Kristin. 2017. "Where's the money coming from for North Korea's nuclear programme?" *South China Morning Post*. Retrieved from https://www.scmp.com/news/china/diplomacy-defence/article/2111427/wheres-money-coming-north-koreas-nuclear-programme.
30. Bueno de Mesquita, Bruce & Smith, Alistair. 2010. "Leader Survival, Revolutions, and the Nature of Government Finance." *American Journal of Political Science* 54: 936–950; Bueno de Mesquita, Bruce & Smith, Alistair. 2011. *A Dictator's Handbook: Why Bad Behavior is Almost Always Good Politics*. New York: Public Affairs. p. 49; Bove, Vincenzo & Rivera, Mauricio. 2015. "Elite Co-optation, Repression, and Coups in Autocracies." *International Interactions* 41 (3): 456; Svolik, Milan. 2009. "Power-Sharing and Leadership Dynamics in Authoritarian Regimes." *American Journal of Political Science* 53 (2): 477–494; Acemoglu, Daron, Robinson, James A. & Verdier, Thierry. 2004. "Kleptocracy and Divide and Rule: A Model of Personal Rule." *Journal of the European Economic Association* 2 (2): 162–192; Egorov, Georgy & Sonin, Konstantin. 2011. "Dictators and Their Viziers: Endogenizing the Loyalty-Competence Trade-Off." *Journal of the European Economic Association* 9 (5): 903–930.
31. McEachern, Patrick. 2010. *Inside the red box: North Korea's post-totalitarian politics*. New York: Columbia University Press; Mahdavi, Paasha & Ishiyama, John. 2019. "Dynamics of the inner elite in dictatorships: Evidence from North Korea." *Comparative Politics*. Retrieved from https://doi.org/10.5129/001041520X15652680065751; Koo, Bon Sang. 2017. "Unique or Common? The Kim Jong Un Regime and Modern Authoritarianism." *North Korean Review* 13 (2): 5–23; Frank, Rudiger & Park, Phillip H. 2012. "From Monolithic Totalitarian to Collective Authoritarian Leadership? Performance-Based Legitimacy and Power Transfer in North Korea." *North Korean Review* 8 (2): 32–49; Wintrobe, Ronald. 2013. "North Korea as a Military Dictatorship." *Peace Economics, Peace Science and Public Policy* 19 (3): 459–471; Myers, Brian Reynolds. 2010. *The Cleanest Race: How North Koreans See themselves and why it matters*. New York: Melville House. Myers, Brian Reynolds. 2017. "What the West gets wrong about North Korea's motives, and why some South Koreans admire the North." *The Conversation*. Retrieved from https://theconversation.com/what-the-west-gets-wrong-about-north-koreas-motives-and-why-some-south-koreans-admire-the-north-83639.

32. Silberstein, Benjamin Katzeff. 2018. "Don't Forget: North Korea Is a Country, Too." *The Diplomat*. Retrieved from https://thediplomat.com/2018/06/dont-forget-north-korea-is-a-country-too/; Myers, Brian Reynolds. 2017. "What the West gets wrong about North Korea's motives, and why some South Koreans admire the North." *The Conversation*. Retrieved from https://theconversation.com/what-the-west-gets-wrong-about-north-koreas-motives-and-why-some-south-koreans-admire-the-north-83639; Myers, Brian Reynolds. 2011. *The Cleanest Race: How North Koreans See themselves and why it matters*. New York: Melville House. Retrieved from https://www.amazon.com/Cleanest-Race-Koreans-Themselves-Matters/dp/1935554344.
33. McEachern, Patrick. 2008. Interest Groups in North Korean Politics. Journal of Asian Studies 8: 235–258. Retrieved from https://www.jstor.org/stable/23418692?seq=1#page_scan_tab_contents; McEachern, Patrick. 2009. *Inside the red box: North Korea's post-totalitarian politics*. Baton Rouge: Louisiana State University and Agricultural and Mechanical College. Retrieved from https://digitalcommons.lsu.edu/cgi/viewcontent.cgi?article=2062&context=gradschool_dissertations.
34. McEachern, Patrick. 2009. *Inside the red box: North Korea's post-totalitarian politics*. City: Louisiana State University and Agricultural and Mechanical College. Retrieved from https://digitalcommons.lsu.edu/cgi/viewcontent.cgi?article=2062&context=gradschool_dissertations.
35. Kim, Youngjun. 2017. Origins of the North Korean Garrison State. New York: Routledge.
36. McEachern, Patrick. 2010. *Inside the red box: North Korea's post-totalitarian politics*. New York: Columbia University Press.
37. Myers, Brian Reynolds. 2010. *The Cleanest Race: How North Koreans See themselves and why it matters*. New York: Melville House.
38. Lipes, Joshua. 2018. "Kim Jong Un Slush Fund 'Running Out' as North Korea Tests Weapons Despite Sanctions." *Radio Free Asia*. Retrieved from https://www.rfa.org/english/news/korea/fund-01252018143318.html; Smith, Nicola. 2018. "Kim Jong-un's 'inheritance dwindling' after expensive missile tests and vanity projects." *The Telegraph*. Retrieved from https://www.telegraph.co.uk/news/2018/01/29/kim-jong-uns-inheritance-dwindling-expensive-missile-tests-vanity/; Lee, Christy. 2019. "Sanctions Threaten North Korea's Old and New Elites." *VOA News*. Retrieved from https://www.voanews.com/east-asia-pacific/sanctions-threaten-north-koreas-old-and-new-elites.
39. U.S. Department of the Treasury. (n.d.) "North Korea Sanctions." Retrieved from https://www.treasury.gov/resource-center/sanctions/Programs/pages/nkorea.aspx.

40. Countering America's Adversaries Through Sanctions Act. H.R.3364. 115th Congress. 2017.
41. Stanton, Joshua, Lee, Sung-Yoon & Klingner, Bruce. 2017. "Getting Tough on North Korea. How to Hit Pyongyang Where It Hurts." *Foreign Affairs.* Retrieved from https://www.foreignaffairs.com/articles/north-korea/2017-04-17/getting-tough-north-korea.
42. Choe, Sang-Hun. 2019. "South Korea Announces $8 Million Aid Package for North." *The New York Times.* Retrieved from https://www.nytimes.com/2019/05/17/world/asia/north-korea-aid-south.html.
43. N.A. April 7, 2018. *China applies its own maximum pressure policy on Pyongyang.* CNBC. https://www.cnbc.com/2018/04/07/china-applies-its-own-maximum-pressure-policy-on-pyongyang.html. Accessed August 14, 2019.
44. World Food Program DPR Korea. (2019). World Food Program DPR Korea 2019–2021. Pyongyang.
45. The Ministry of Unification, *Policy on North Korean Defectors*, 2019.
46. Yonhap. 2019. "Trump says 'lot of things going on' regarding NK, raises prospects of 'major rebuild'." *The Korea Herald.* Retrieved from http://www.koreaherald.com/view.php?ud=20191022000142.
47. Kim, Jaewon. 2019. "Ex-North Korean diplomat says Kim will never give up nuclear arms." *Nikkei Asian Review.* Retrieved from https://asia.nikkei.com/Politics/Trump-Kim-Summit/Ex-North-Korean-diplomat-says-Kim-will-never-give-up-nuclear-arms.
48. Smith. Nicola. 2018. "North Korea warns Kim will not give up nuclear weapons until US removes threat." *The Telegraph.* Retrieved from https://www.telegraph.co.uk/news/2018/12/21/north-korea-warns-will-not-give-nuclear-weapons-us-removes-threat/.
49. Richardson, Davis. 2019. "North Korea 'Unlikely to Give Up' Nuclear Arsenal, Says National Security Team." *Observer.* Retrieved from https://observer.com/2019/01/north-korea-nuclear-arsenal-national-security-team/.

Bibliography

Acemoglu, Daron, Robinson, James A. & Verdier, Thierry. 2004. "Kleptocracy and Divide and Rule: A Model of Personal Rule." *Journal of the European Economic Association* 2 (2): 162–192.

Armitage, Richard L. 1999. "A Comprehensive Approach to North Korea." *Institute for National Strategic Studies.* Retrieved from http://www.globalsecurity.org/wmd/library/news/dprk/1999/forum159.html.

Author. "North Korea Trade Arms Funds Nuclear-Bomb Work, UN Panel Says." 2010. *Bloomberg.* Retrieved from http://www.bloomberg.com/apps/news?pid=newsarchive&sid=aqoIAn3ecoic.

Bader, Jeffrey A. 2017. "Why deterring and containing North Korea is our least bad option." *Brookings*. Retrieved from https://www.brookings.edu/blog/order-from-chaos/2017/08/08/why-deterring-and-containing-north-korea-is-our-least-bad-option/.

Bang, Chan Young, 1995. *The Democratic People's Republic of Korea at a crossroad*. Seoul: Park Young-sa. pp. 99, 232–233.

Battacharjee, Anjali & Salama, Sammy. 2003. *Libya and Nonproliferation*. Monterey, CA: Center for Nonproliferation Studies.

Blackwill, Robert & Carnesale, Albert. 1993. *New Nuclear Nations: Consequences of U.S. Policy*. New York: Council on Foreign Relations Press.

Bove, Vincenzo & Rivera, Mauricio. 2015. "Elite Co-optation, Repression, and Coups in Autocracies." *International Interactions* 41 (3): 456.

Braut-Hegghammer, Maalfrid. 2009. "Libya's Nuclear Intentions: Ambition and Ambivalence." *Center Contemporary Conflict*. Retrieved from http://www.nps.edu/Academics/centers/ccc/publications/OnlineJournal/2009/Apr/braut-hegghammerApr09.pdf.

Bueno de Mesquita, Bruce & Smith, Alistair. 2010. "Leader Survival, Revolutions, and the Nature of Government Finance." *American Journal of Political Science* 54: 936–950.

Bueno de Mesquita, Bruce & Smith, Alistair. 2011. *A Dictator's Handbook: Why Bad Behavior is Almost Always Good Politics*. New York: Public Affairs. p. 49.

Buncombe, Andrew. 2018a. "North Korea says there is 'no way' it will give up nuclear weapons without trust." *Independent*. Retrieved from https://www.independent.co.uk/news/world/asia/north-korea-latest-nuclear-weapons-disarm-united-nations-trust-us-sanctions-a8561371.html.

Buncombe, Andrew. 2018b. "North Korea says there is 'no way' it will give up nuclear weapons without trust." *Independent*. Retrieved from https://www.independent.co.uk/news/world/asia/north-korea-latest-nuclear-weapons-disarm-united-nations-trust-us-sanctions-a8561371.html.

Buzan, Barry & Waever, Ole. 2003. *Region and Powers*. New York: Cambridge University Press.

Cha, Victor & Collins, Lisa. 2018. "The Markets: Private Economy and Capitalism in North Korea?" Beyond Parallel. Retrieved from https://beyondparallel.csis.org/markets-private-economy-capitalism-north-korea/.

Choe, Sang-Hun. 2019. "South Korea Announces $8 Million Aid Package for North." *The New York Times*. Retrieved from https://www.nytimes.com/2019/05/17/world/asia/north-korea-aid-south.html.

Chotiner, Isaac. 2019. "The early life of Kim Jong Un." *The New Yorker*. Retrieved from https://www.newyorker.com/news/q-and-a/the-early-life-of-kim-jong-un.

Countering America's Adversaries Through Sanctions Act. H.R.3364. 115th Congress. 2017.

Cirincione, Joseph, Wolfsthal, Jon & Rajkumar, Miriam. 2002. *Deadly Arsenals, Tracking Weapons of Mass Destruction*. Washington, DC: Carnegie Endowment for International Peace.

Crincione, Joseph, Wolfsthal, Jon B. & Rajkumar, Miriam. 2005. *Deadly Arsenals: Nuclear, Biological, and Chemical Threats Second Edition*. Washington, DC: Carnegie Endowment for International Peace.

Daily NK. 2018. "Report: The Creation of the North Korean Market System." Retrieved from https://www.dailynk.com/english/notices/?mod=document&uid=68.

Dekleva, Kenneth B. 2019. "A Hypothetical Letter from Chairman Kim Jong Un to President Donald Trump." *38 North*. Retrieved from https://www.38north.org/2019/06/kdekleva060719/.

Dong, Yong-seung. 1997. "The Impact of the Black Market Spread on the North Korean Economy." [Amsijang hwaksani bukhangyeongjeaae michineun yeonghyang]. *Monthly Samsung Economic Group*.

Dty, Paul & Flank, Steven. 1993. "Arms Control for New Nuclear Nations." In Robert Blackwill & Albert Carnesale, *New Nuclear Nations: Consequences of U.S. Policy*. New York: Council on Foreign Relations Press.

Egorov, Georgy & Sonin, Konstantin. 2011. "Dictators and Their Viziers: Endogenizing the Loyalty-Competence Trade-Off." *Journal of the European Economic Association* 9 (5): 903–930.

Everard, John. 2012. *Only Beautiful, Please: A British Diplomat in North Korea*. Baltimore: The Brooking Institution.

Fifield, Anna. 2019. *The Great Successor: The Divinely Perfect Destiny of Brilliant Comrade Kim Jong Un*. New York: Public Affairs. p. 104.

Frank, Rudiger & Park, Phillip H. 2012. "From Monolithic Totalitarian to Collective Authoritarian Leadership? Performance-Based Legitimacy and Power Transfer in North Korea." *North Korean Review* 8 (2): 32–49.

Geleskul, Elena. 1987. "The History of the Libyan Nuclear Program: The Reasons for Failure." *Security Index* 15 (2): 139–145.

Grossman, Gregory. 1977. "The 'Second Economy' of USSR." *Problems of Communism* 26 (5): 25–40.

Hecker, Siegfried S. 2010. *Special Report: A Return Trip to North Korea's Yongbyon Nuclear Complex*. Washington, DC: Korea Economic Institute.

Huang, Kristin. 2017. "Where's the money coming from for North Korea's nuclear programme?" *South China Morning Post*. Retrieved from https://www.scmp.com/news/china/diplomacy-defence/article/2111427/wheres-money-coming-north-koreas-nuclear-programme.

Huh Man-ho. 2008. *Reform of North Korea. Openness and Human Rights [Bukhanui gaehyeokgaebanggwainkwon]*. Seoul: Master Culture History. p. 36.

Huh, Man-ho. 2008. *Reform of North Korea. Openness and Human Rights [Bukhanui gaehyeokgaebanggwainkwon]*. Seoul: Master Culture History. p. 39.

Jang, Jin-sung. 2014. *Dear Leader*. London: Ebury Publishing.

Jeong, Se-jin. 2000. *From Plan to Market: Political Economy of the North Korean regime [Gyehuyeseo sijanguro: Bukhan chejebyendong jeongchi kyungje yengu]*. Seoul: Hanul Academy. pp. 20–32.

Jeong-ho, Lee & Chan, Minnie. 2018. "Kim Jong-un will use nuclear weapons to push for more from West, ex-South Korean negotiator says." *South China Morning Post*. Retrieved from https://www.scmp.com/news/china/diplomacy-defence/article/2143585/kim-jong-un-will-use-nuclear-weapons-push-more-west-ex.

Jones-Rooy, Andrea & Prusher, Ilene. 2018. "Even Dictators Like Kim Jong Un Need To Keep Some People Happy." *FiveThirtyEight*. Retrieved from https://fivethirtyeight.com/features/even-dictators-like-kim-jong-un-need-to-keep-some-people-happy/.

Jongwha, Lee. 2019. "A Practical Approach to North Korean Denuclearization." *Project Syndicate*. Retrieved from https://www.project-syndicate.org/commentary/north-korea-denuclearization-inter-korean-cooperation-by-lee-jong-wha-2019-05.

Joong-Ang Ilbo reports. 2017. "Korea's economic assistance should be reformed and opened by the U.S. government." [Hangukgyungjeajiwon, michejeabojangeurobukgyehteokgaebanghaeya]. Retrieved from https://news.joins.com/article/22074358.

Kang, David C. 2018. "Why should North Korea give up its nuclear weapons?" *The New York Times*. Retrieved from https://www.nytimes.com/2018/08/22/opinion/north-korea-nuclear-trump.html.

Kim, Byung-Yeon. 2017a. *Unveiling The North Korean Economy: Collapse and Transition*. Cambridge: Cambridge University Press.

Kim, Jaewon. 2019. "Ex-North Korean diplomat says Kim will never give up nuclear arms." *Nikkei Asian Review*. Retrieved from https://asia.nikkei.com/Politics/Trump-Kim-Summit/Ex-North-Korean-diplomat-says-Kim-will-never-give-up-nuclear-arms.

Kim, Suki. 2014. *Without you, there is no us: my time with the sons of North Korea's elites*. New York: Crown Publishers.

Kim, Youngjun. 2017b. *Origins of the North Korean Garrison State*. New York: Routledge.

Koo, Bon Sang. 2017. "Unique or Common? The Kim Jong Un Regime and Modern Authoritarianism." *North Korean Review* 13 (2): 5–23.

Kyodo News. 2019. "Kim not giving up nukes, North Korea military officers likely told." Retrieved from https://english.kyodonews.net/news/2019/06/56ba48cc7005-kim-not-giving-up-nukes-n-korea-military-officers-likely-told.html.

Lee, Christy. 2019. "Sanctions Threaten North Korea's Old and New Elites." *VOA News*. Retrieved from https://www.voanews.com/east-asia-pacific/sanctions-threaten-north-koreas-old-and-new-elites.

Lipes, Joshua. 2018. "Kim Jong Un Slush Fund 'Running Out' as North Korea Tests Weapons Despite Sanctions." *Radio Free Asia*. Retrieved from https://www.rfa.org/english/news/korea/fund-01252018143318.html.

Mahdavi, Paasha & Ishiyama, John. 2017. "International political, personal rule and changes in the elite in North Korea." Paper prepared for the 2017 International Studies Association. Hong Kong.

Mahdavi, Paasha & Ishiyama, John. 2019. "Dynamics of the inner elite in dictatorships: Evidence from North Korea." *Comparative Politics*. Retrieved from https://doi.org/10.5129/001041520X15652680065751.

Manyin, Mark E. & Nikitin, Mary Beth D. 2008. *US Assistance to North Korea*. Washington, DC: CRS Report.

Martin, Bradley K. 2019a. "How the US president could earn his Nobel." *Asia Times*. Retrieved from https://www.asiatimes.com/2019/06/article/how-the-us-president-could-earn-his-nobel/.

Martin, Bradley K. 2019b. "How the US president could earn his Nobel". *Asia Times*. Retrieved from https://www.asiatimes.com/2019/06/article/how-the-us-president-could-earn-his-nobel/.

McEachern, Patrick. 2008. Interest Groups in North Korean Politics. *Journal of Asian Studies* 8: 235–258. Retrieved from https://www.jstor.org/stable/23418692?seq=1#page_scan_tab_contents.

McEachern, Patrick. 2010. *Inside the red box: North Korea's post-totalitarian politics*. New York: Columbia University Press.

Myers, Brian Reynolds. 2010. *The Cleanest Race: How North Koreans See themselves and why it matters*. New York: Melville House.

Myers, Brian Reynolds. 2017. "What the West gets wrong about North Korea's motives, and why some South Koreans admire the North." *The Conversation*. Retrieved from https://theconversation.com/what-the-west-gets-wrong-about-north-koreas-motives-and-why-some-south-koreans-admire-the-north-83639.

Nee, Victor & Lian, Peng. 1994. "Sleeping with the enemy: why communications love the market." *Theory and Society* 23 (2): 253–296.

NKBD Database Center for North Korean Human Rights. Findings. Retrieved from http://www.nkdb.org/en/database/findings.php.

Park, Soon-sung and others. 2009. "North Korean defectors in the process of defection and resettlement." [Talbuk yeosunguitalbukmit jungchak gwajeongaeseouiinkwonchimhaesiltaejosha]. *National Human Rights Commission of Korea*. p. 53.

Pyongyang. 2003. "Commercial Holy Place of the Democratic People's Republic of Korea," [Joshunminjujuui inmingonghwaguk sangeopjishi]. No. 48, May 20, 2003.

Richardson, Davis. 2019. "North Korea 'Unlikely to Give Up' Nuclear Arsenal, Says National Security Team." *Observer*. Retrieved from https://observer.com/2019/01/north-korea-nuclear-arsenal-national-security-team/.

Schophlin, George. 1993. *Politics in Eastern Europe, 1945–1992*. Oxford: Blackwell Publishers.

Shevardnadze, Eduard. 1991. *The Future Belongs to Freedom*. New York: The Free Press. pp. 57–58.

Silberstein, Benjamin Katzeff. 2018. "Don't Forget: North Korea Is a Country, Too." *The Diplomat*. Retrieved from https://thediplomat.com/2018/06/dont-forget-north-korea-is-a-country-too/.

Smith, Nicola. 2018a. "Kim Jong Un's 'inheritance dwindling' after expensive missile tests and vanity projects." *The Telegraph*. Retrieved from https://www.telegraph.co.uk/news/2018/01/29/kim-jong-uns-inheritance-dwindling-expensive-missile-tests-vanity/.

Smith, Nicola. 2018b. "North Korea warns it will not give up nuclear weapons until US removes 'threat'." *The Telegraph*. Retrieved from https://www.telegraph.co.uk/news/2018/12/21/north-korea-warns-will-not-give-nuclear-weapons-us-removes-threat/.

Smith, Nicola. 2018c. "North Korea warns Kim will not give up nuclear weapons until US removes threat." *The Telegraph*. Retrieved from https://www.telegraph.co.uk/news/2018/12/21/north-korea-warns-will-not-give-nuclear-weapons-us-removes-threat/.

Song, Wonjun & Wright, Joseph. 2018. "The North Korean Autocracy in Comparative Perspective." *Journal of East Asian Studies* 18 (2): 157–180.

Squassoni, Sharon & Feickert, Andrew. 2004. *Disarming Libya: Weapons of Mass Destruction*. Washington, DC: CRS Report for Congress.

Squassoni, Sharon. 2004. *Globalizing Cooperative Threat Reduction: A Survey of Options*. Washington, DC: CRS Report for Congress.

Stanton, Joshua, Lee, Sung-Yoon & Klingner, Bruce. 2017. "Getting Tough on North Korea. How to Hit Pyongyang Where It Hurts." *Foreign Affairs*. Retrieved from https://www.foreignaffairs.com/articles/north-korea/2017-04-17/getting-tough-north-korea.

Stricker, Andrea & Albright, David. 2019a. "How North Korea can be convinced to give up nuclear weapons." *NK News*. Retrieved from https://www.nknews.org/2019/01/how-north-korea-can-be-convinced-to-give-up-nuclear-weapons/.

Stricker, Andrea & Albright, David. 2019b. "How North Korea can be convinced to give up nuclear weapons." *NK News*. Retrieved from https://www.nknews.org/2019/01/how-north-korea-can-be-convinced-to-give-up-nuclear-weapons/.

Svolik, Milan. 2009. "Power-Sharing and Leadership Dynamics in Authoritarian Regimes." *American Journal of Political Science* 53 (2): 477–494.

The National Committee of North Korea. 2016. "Summary of the North Korea Sanctions and Policy Enhancement Act of 2016." Retrieved from https://www.ncnk.org/resources/publications/HR757_Summary_Final.pdf.

Tongilwon, "North Korean dog '91'"[Bukhangaeyo](Seoul: Tongilwon, 1990), p. 238.

U.S. Department of the Treasury. n.d. "North Korea Sanctions." Retrieved from https://www.treasury.gov/resource-center/sanctions/Programs/pages/nkorea.aspx.

US Congress. 1996a. "Iran and Libya Sanctions Act of 1996." *House of Representatives.* Retrieved from http://www.fas.org/irp/congress/1996_cr/h960618b.html.

US Congress. 1996b. Iran and Libya Sanctions Act of 1996. Retrieved from http://www.fas.org/irp/congress/1996_cr/h960618b.html.

Washington, DC: US Arms Control and Disarmament Agency. 1998. *Signatories and Parties to the Treaty on the Non-Proliferation of Nuclear Weapons.*

Willis, James. 2019. "Readers React: Why Kim Jong Un will never give up North Korea's nukes: Moammar Kadafi." *Los Angeles Times.* Retrieved from https://www.latimes.ckom/opinion/readersreact/la-ol-le-north-korea-kim-jong-un-kadafi-20190301-story.html.

Wintrobe, Ronald. 2013. "North Korea as a Military Dictatorship." *Peace Economics, Peace Science and Public Policy* 19 (3): 459–471.

Wit, Joel S. & Sokolsky, Richard. 2019. "Memo to Donald Trump: It's Time to End-Run Your Advisers on North Korea." *38 North.* Retrieved from https://www.38north.org/2019/05/jwitrsokolsky052219/.

World Politics Review. 2019. "Why North Korea Denuclearization Is Such a Long Shot." Retrieved from https://www.worldpoliticsreview.com/insights/27952/why-north-korea-denuclearization-is-such-a-long-shot.

Yang Moon-soo. 2014. *Economy and Society in the Kim Jong-un Era: New Relations Between the State and the Market [Kimjeongeunshidaeuigyeongjeawasahoe: gukgawasijangui saerowoon gwangye].* "Chapter 10. Marketization and Gender of North Korea." Seoul: Hanul Academy. pp. 302–303.

Yonhap. 2019a. "N. Korea changes constitution to make Kim Jong-un official head of state." *The Korea Herald.* Retrieved from http://www.koreaherald.com/view.php?ud=20190711000731.

Yonhap. 2019b. "NK's official newspaper urges stepped-up resistance against US sanctions." *The Korea Herald.* Retrieved from http://www.koreaherald.com/common/newsprint.php?ud=20191021000198.

Yonhap. 2019c. "Trump says 'lot of things going on' regarding NK, raises prospects of 'major rebuild'." *The Korea Herald.* Retrieved from http://www.koreaherald.com/view.php?ud=20191022000142.

Yuwen, Deng. 2018. "Why Kim Jong Un's promise of a nuclear-free North Korea should not be trusted." *South China Morning Post.* Retrieved from https://www.scmp.com/comment/insight-opinion/article/2144623/why-kim-jong-uns-promise-nuclear-free-north-korea-should-not.

CHAPTER 4

Economic Modernization Beyond Denuclearization

1 Introduction

In Chap. 4, we arrive at the culmination of the main tenet of this book—what conditions must be satisfied and which measures must be taken in order for the DPRK to survive without nuclear weapons as an economically prosperous, normalized state. This chapter addresses the essential attributes of how North Korea can secure a road to a "bright future" through radical, market-oriented reform and opening with spectacular economic growth in return for the dismantlement of its nuclear weapons program. In Chap. 2, I illustrated the manner in which the North Korean economy evolved from its roots in traditional socialism to the dysfunctional system that we see today. This occurred through its adherence to the fundamental principles of socialism, onto which *Juche* ideology was grafted by Kim Il Sung, and the demise of the Soviet Union during Kim Jong Il's reign, causing North Korea's loss of crucial socialist trading partners and allies. In addition, the Arduous March and continuous process of unofficial marketization from below that has expanded under the leadership of Kim Jong Un played a significant role, as well. Following this detailed explanation, in Chap. 3, I established the foundational factors of the prevailing North Korean system that have enabled the regime to survive thus far, but are in a state of such erosion that they no longer serve to protect North Korea.

C. Y. Bang, *Transition beyond Denuclearisation*,
https://doi.org/10.1007/978-981-15-4316-6_4

1.1 *Necessary Conditions for Survival*

As discussed in Chap. 3, the nuclear weapons program provides Kim Jong Un not only with a credible deterrence measure against real and imagined U.S. military threat but also with a major source of legitimacy as the fulfiller of Kim Il Sung's mandate. Because of the integral role nuclear capability plays in cementing the security of the regime, any denuclearization proposal that stands a chance at Kim Jong Un's acceptance must satisfy the following set of conditions.

In order to convince the DPRK, the stakeholders must put forth a policy that involves the following:

1. Lifting of all military and economic threat and pressure, including but not limited to internationally-imposed sanctions, joint U.S.-South Korean military exercises, deployment of modern weapons systems and diplomatic isolation;
2. Security guarantees from the U.S., South Korea, and Japan, as well as reassurances of alliances with China and Russia;
   - A peace treaty between the North and the South;
   - Guarantees of a future "one nation, two different systems" framework and that neither party will seek coercive political integration; and
   - Radical reduction of military armament in both the North and the South.
3. Allocation of an economic development fund, at least $30 billion annually—$10 billion in cash and $20 billion in the form of vouchers—over a period of 10 years for a total of $300 billion along with assistance from the stakeholders in securing additional loans from global organizations like the World Bank and the IMF.

1.2 *Sufficient Conditions for Survival*

The provisions from the five stakeholders stated above represent only the necessary conditions to denuclearization; they do not meet the sufficient conditions necessary for survival. Dynamic and sustained economic development can only be achieved if North Korea can successfully open and integrate with the world economy. However, this is a feat that can only be realized if it is first preceded by transformation of the distorted socialist economy into a market socialist system through radical reform. For genuine opening and reform to be implemented and thus lay the foundation for unparalleled growth, Kim Jong Un needs a well-conceived blueprint for modernization that fulfills the following sufficient conditions:

1. Replacement of the current, distorted economic system with an efficient one, based on a market-socialist framework and adapted to the peculiarities of the North Korean situation;
2. Achievement of an average minimum GDP growth rate of 10% per annum over the 10-year period of the development fund's provision;
3. A well-conceived, viable plan for development, involving allocation of funds secured from the stakeholders and the introduction of an expert committee to guide throughout opening and reform; and
4. Bold leadership demonstrated through chairing of the expert committee.

1.3 The U.S. Point of View vs. the Stakeholders

From the vantage point of the nations that bear the greatest consequences of the UNSC sanctions—namely Russia, China, and South Korea—the denuclearization of North Korea should not come as a result of the demise of the regime. On the contrary, denuclearization must enable North Korea's development into an economically vibrant, normalized country through the implementation of tangible market-oriented reform and transformation of the regime. For the stakeholders, survival without nuclear weapons must bring peace and prosperity accompanied by the emergence of the DPRK as a new economic power in Northeast Asia that integrates with the world economy and contributes to sustaining a regional security balance that does not tilt in favor of the U.S.

The current policy objective pursued by the Trump administration, which has singularly prioritized the dismantlement of the nuclear weapons programme without addressing the issue of survival with economic development, is inconsistent with the views of the other stakeholders. Because of this dissonance between the interests and concerns of the stakeholders, the U.S. has consistently failed to put forth a policy for denuclearization. Any policy that utilizes threat alone to coerce the DPRK into giving up its nuclear weapons is doomed to fail—provoking North Korea to armed response or instigating the collapse of the regime altogether. This is not a scenario that any of the remaining stakeholders will support. Survival without nuclear weapons with sustained economic development through reform and opening, however, would be a win-win scenario for all parties involved, transforming the DPRK into a viable state, integrated with the world economy, paving the road to permanent peace, signaling that threat is no longer posed to the U.S.

It should be duly noted that neither the U.S. nor any other single stakeholder nation possesses all of the "sticks" and "carrots" necessary to persuade North Korea to embrace modernization in exchange for denuclearization. If the U.S. hopes to lead the stakeholders in resolving the nuclear crisis, policy makers must seek to align their divergent concerns and interest in the formulation of a shared policy. On the basis of this shared policy, the five nations must pool their collective resources to form a proposal that ensures a "bright future" for North Korea through rapid economic development in exchange for denuclearization.

1.4 Transaction and Transformation

Any deal for denuclearization that involves a simple trade for security guarantees and development funds will never succeed in establishing North Korea as a prosperous, viable state through dynamic and sustained economic development. In order to implement economic opening, two stipulations must be ensured: first, that transformation into a market socialist system takes place, and second, that the DPRK can successfully integrate with the world economy. There will be no amicable solution nor survival of Kim Jong Un's regime without a strategic plan for economic development with the aim of transforming into a "market socialist" system.

Therefore, any package deal presented by the stakeholders must require not only transaction, i.e. permanent dismantlement of the nuclear weapons program (in exchange for security guarantees), but also transformation (traded for economic compensation)—a fundamental paradigm shift in the nature of the regime. Such transformation must involve a change from hostile foreign policy to amicable, normalized relations. This is the only path towards establishing a "bright future" for North Korea that enables the regime to achieve dynamic, sustained economic growth through reform of the distorted system, transformation into a market socialist economy with the introduction of amicable foreign policy.

1.5 A Deal North Korea Cannot Refuse

Thus, Chap. 4 explores the question that the U.S. and other stakeholders ought to ask: not "What punitive measures should be taken to coerce the DPRK into accepting denuclearization?" but "What will it take for the DPRK to emerge as an economically prosperous state after the abandonment of nuclear weapons?" Essentially, if a policy put forth by the five members of the Six-party Talks is to be successful, the U.S. must take the lead in formulating a shared policy that is in accord with the interests and concerns of all of the stakeholders. This policy must take the essential form of an economic package deal with security guarantees to entice the DPRK to embrace denuclearization, leading to the road to a "bright future"—a deal that North Korea could not possibly refuse.

In this way, they can deliver the leadership a new source of legitimacy and enable him to be recorded in history as a great leader who founded his own legacy by building an economically-prosperous country against overwhelming odds, rather than as a ruler trapped in their ancestors' shadow. What follows is a detailed explanation of this very policy recommendation.

2 Necessary Conditions: Cost-Benefit Analysis and the Win-Win Scenario

2.1 The Rationality of Kim Jong Un

Kim Jong Un is a rational leader, and having understood that the chances for regime survival with nuclear weapons program are dim, his interests have already begun to shift from the development of weapons of mass destruction to improving the welfare of the people.

A week before his birthday in 2018, Kim Jong Un repeatedly emphasized economic development, and he mentioned it 39 times during his 2019 New Year's Day speech. During the address, he asserted that North Korea would "no longer make, test, use or proliferate nuclear weapons."[1] In addition, on April 20, 10 days after the Supreme People's Assembly, the Central Committee of the Party announced that North Korea would terminate its nuclear arms production project and concentrate its efforts on economic construction, announcing an end to the *byongjin* line.[2]

At the time of his visit to Pyongyang leading up to the inter-Korean summit in 2018, then-CIA director Mike Pompeo directly asked Kim

Jong Un whether he truly intended to give up nuclear weapons. Chairman Kim answered: "I am a husband and a father of children. I do not want my children to live with nuclear weapons for life."[3] After the June 2018 summit in Singapore with U.S. President Donald J. Trump, Trump noted that Kim Jong Un was a smart negotiator who had been "able to run" his country despite inheriting leadership at a young age.[4]

By applying analytical reasoning to Kim Jong Un's public statements and the rapidly deteriorating socioeconomic conditions in contemporary North Korea, I have come to the conclusion that he would make the rational decision to recognize that the only path towards survival is by giving up nuclear weapons in exchange for economic modernization. In view of this record, the U.S. with the support of the stakeholders can genuinely persuade Kim Jong Un to make a choice between two contrasting options—acceptance of a "bright future" in return for denuclearization or rejection in favor of maintaining the current system and nuclear weapons. I am certain that, in the past, he has been prepared to make the rational choice.

2.2 *The Collective Threats and Promises*

Thus far, the concerted efforts of the U.S. to dismantle the North Korean nuclear weapons program have failed consistently because they have not clearly enunciated a shared policy objective that all of the remaining stakeholders can faithfully execute. Russia, South Korea and China have made clear that the denuclearization of North Korea cannot come at the expense of the collapse of the regime. It should be noted that, although a North Korea armed with nuclear weapons is against the security interests of all of the stakeholder nations, the stakeholder's views on how to achieve denuclearization diverge.

In his work, *Threats and Promises: The Pursuit of International Influence*, James W. Davis introduces the concept of "threats" and "promises," also commonly referred to as "sticks" and "carrots" or "costs" and "benefits," which I apply here in the formulation of a policy for the members of the Six-party Talks. The collective stakeholders have a variety of threats and promises in their arsenal, but they will only succeed in achieving a peaceful settlement if the U.S. can first identify all of the "sticks" and "carrots" at hand and effectively apply them towards the achievement of a common goal.

From the side of the "sticks," or "threats," there is an array of means that can be appropriated by the U.S. and other stakeholders to exert pressure on North Korea, both collectively and individually. These include, but are not limited to, joint military exercises, censure for human rights violations, diplomatic isolation, secondary boycotts, inspections on international waters, blacklisting and punitive measures. Of all the possible forms of pressure, however, the most effective means of exerting threat is by economic sanctions.

What the U.S. must recognize in formulating a shared policy is that, although the U.S. may apply unilateral sanctions against the regime, this tool can only be effectively applied collectively, through the cooperation of all of the stakeholder nations through the U.N. Security Council. It should be noted that the only country capable of exerting fatal force against the DPRK through the use of sanctions is China. However, if sanctions are implemented with the objective of toppling the regime, the stakeholders, especially China and Russia, will never faithfully execute them. The U.S. must align their policy objective with the interests of the other stakeholders in order to exert a sufficiently forceful threat against the DPRK, persuading North Korea that the costs of retaining nuclear weapons would be destructive enough to accept the benefits of denuclearization.

As discussed in detail in Chap. 3, the U.S. can offer "carrots" in the form of security guarantees by putting an end to joint military exercises with South Korea and ultimately withdrawing from the peninsula upon complete dismantlement, eventually establishing normalized diplomatic relations. South Korea can enter into a peace treaty with the North that would guarantee a "one country, two systems" framework, while also bearing the major burden of the provision of an economic development fund. China and Russia can reaffirm treaties, while Japan provides reparations for colonial rule and normalizes relations with the DPRK. The most important carrot, however, is an economic development fund for rapid modernization, provided by the collective stakeholders. In addition, to boost economic growth, the stakeholders can lift crippling internationally-imposed sanctions and give their support to North Korea to secure additional development funds from international monetary organizations.

Needless to say, not all of these "carrots" are at the disposal of the U.S. Therefore, it is of paramount importance that, upon identifying the promises that can be used, the U.S. recognizes that it cannot offer all of the necessary "carrots" on its own. Instead, to achieve a peaceful resolution, the U.S. must secure the unyielding commitment of all of the remaining stakeholder nations to mobilize their collective promises. This is the only way to optimize the applications of the "sticks" and "carrots" to ensure denuclearization and the establishment of peace and prosperity on the Korean Peninsula.

2.3 *Cost-Benefit Analysis*

Thus, a cost-benefit analysis through the application of "threats" and "promises" is a powerful tool the stakeholders have at their disposal. In order to optimize the chances of a peaceful settlement, rational calculation dictates that the higher the benefit and more prohibitive the cost, the greater the chances of an amicable resolution. In the case of North Korea, this means that the benefits of modernization must genuinely entice the regime to abandon all nuclear capabilities. In other words, the DPRK must be convinced that it actually has a better chance of survival as a state if it relinquishes its nuclear programs. It is my conviction that Kim Jong Un is a rational actor who is more than capable of making the logical decision to accept the benefits of economic modernization—but only if these benefits far outweigh the costs that would be suffered if he chose to retain nuclear weapons.

In order to maximize the benefit that the stakeholders can put forth, there are a number of critical variables which much be taken into account. The size of compensation the stakeholders should offer is tied directly to these factors, the first being how an economic development fund, contributed by the stakeholders, would be put to use. These funds must be directed to the implementation of reform and opening of the North Korean economy based on a market-socialist model. Second, the target minimum average economic growth rate per annum must be sufficiently high, and the length of the deal adequately long, to ensure spectacular, sustained modernization. Third, these funds directed to economic modernization of the DPRK must also assure a mutually favorable benefit for the economies of the participating stakeholder nations. Fourth, North Korea's disarmament must extend beyond the nuclear weapons program to encompass all weapons of mass destruction, including all chemical weapons and intercontinental missile systems. Finally, to ensure the maximum benefit from the stakeholders, the new source of legitimacy gained by Kim Jong Un must be credible—at least doubling the living standards of the people within seven years of embarking upon economic reform and opening.

Exerting the greatest cost possible, on the other hand, is contingent upon the policy goals of the U.S., as explained above. The U.S. must take the lead in uniting the stakeholder nations over a shared policy, aimed at providing North Korea with a genuine opportunity to pave the road to a "bright future." The stakeholders must align to faithfully implement all of the "sticks" available to them collectively in order to convince Kim Jong Un that the cost of retaining nuclear weapons would be detrimental, while the benefit of accepting denuclearization would offer a chance for survival through economic modernization. Thus, a shared policy must be beneficial to all parties involved in order to succeed.

The past 20 years of policies aimed at the North Korean nuclear crisis have singularly failed because they have ignored the "carrots" they could offer Kim Jong Un and, instead, focused solely on the exertion of "sticks." On its current path, the escalation of sanctions imposed by the international community will eventually become unbearable for North Korea, forcing the regime into an extreme situation: either accept regime collapse or seek an exit option, the former being almost entirely improbable and the latter signaling armed provocation that could have disastrous geopolitical consequences for the region at large. In order to avoid such scenarios, the five stakeholder nations must align under a shared policy that genuinely offers the DPRK a chance at survival through the immense benefits of economic modernization.

In approaching the peaceful dismantlement of the North Korean nuclear weapons program, then, the objective must shift from pressuring the regime into denuclearization to enticing Kim Jong Un to accept the benefits provided by economic modernization. The U.S. must take the lead in crafting such a shared policy while acknowledging the interests of all parties involved. With the conditions articulated, and the stakeholders working toward a cohesive and common policy framework, Kim Jong Un will have a choice: accept the benefits of denuclearization and economic modernization or continue its belligerency and suffer the costs of state collapse. One choice will pave the way for peace and prosperity in Northeast Asia. The other will usher in years of instability and anguish (Fig. 4.1).

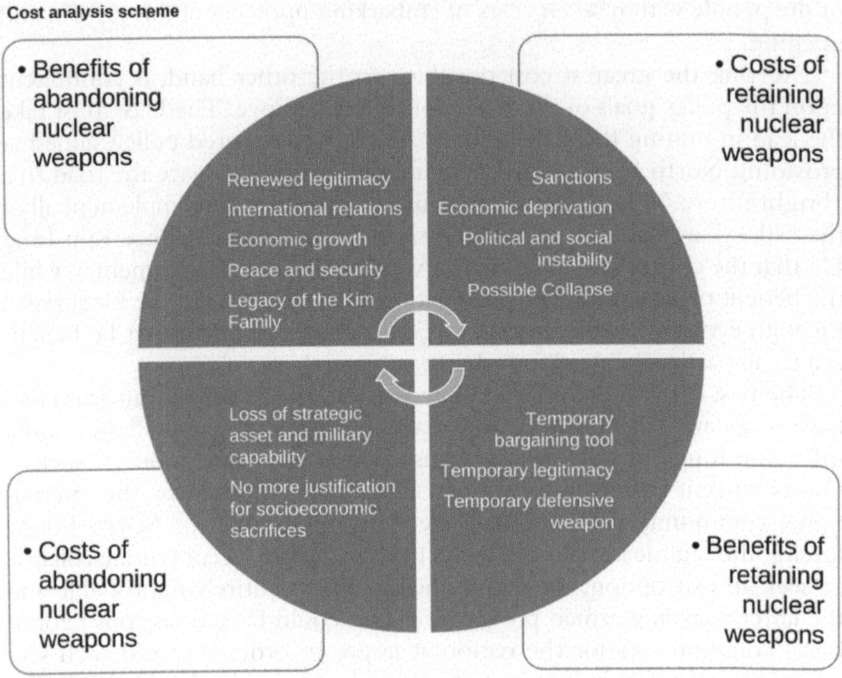

Fig. 4.1 Represents the cost-benefit calculation that Kim Jong Un must conduct in his decision making

3 Necessary Preconditions for North Korean Modernization: Transformation to Market Socialism and Integration with the World Economy

3.1 The Necessity of System Reform for Economic Modernization

The current economic state of North Korea is antithetical to the idea of economic modernization. Its socioeconomic system is, by all intents and purposes, akin to that of a feudalistic state, rather than one of a modern market economy. This state of economic backwardness is characterized by a complete lack of economic and financial institutions, transparency, access to credit and ability to generate wealth and to use and renew all forms of capital, not to mention business entities that operate without legal sanction. Economic modernization is, in a nutshell, all that North Korea lacks at the moment: a credible banking system, a credit circuit, monetary reserves, transparent and efficient bureaucracy, and reliable institutions. Without these institutions in place, economic modernization cannot succeed, even with security guarantees and the lifting of sanctions.

Before any attempts at modernization or opening can take place, the DPRK must implement market-oriented economic reforms. As a closed state, as famously asserted by Deng Xiaoping, cannot achieve economic modernization,[5] it is of paramount importance that opening is preceded by reform measures to ensure its successful implementation.

Namely, the extreme distortions of the North Korean economy, explored in Chap. 2, must be addressed in order to establish an efficient market system. Opening is more than just a short-term influx of development funds or aid; the opening of the DPRK must entail full integration with the world economy and its transformation into a normalized, friendly trade partner. In order to do so, Kim Jong Un must make the decision to reform the regime—both economically and politically—before opening can take place. Hostile foreign policy must be replaced by amicable relations in order to integrate and attract foreign capital to the North Korean emerging market.

Thus, there are three conditions to be met and implemented for modernization to have a genuine chance at success:

- Market-oriented system reform
- Friendly, non-aggressive foreign policy implementation
- Opening for global economy and integration

In order to achieve high, sustained growth, North Korea must introduce a viable economic model for the transformation of the distorted socialist system into an efficient, market-socialist economy. Before we can explore the composition of such a model for the DPRK, we must first turn to the lessons that can be learned from the experiences of other formalist nations—namely, Vietnam and China.

3.2 Pertinent Lessons from the Experience of Vietnam

Many experts compare the situation of the DPRK with Vietnam's economic development model, which has achieved an impressive 6.7% annual average growth over a 10-year period. The view that the DPRK should deem Vietnam as a benchmark case seems to be gradually gaining momentum.[6] Among those who share this perspective is US Secretary of State Mike Pompeo, who paid a visit to Hanoi in July 2018 and stated that North Korea can emulate the economic development model of Vietnam and achieve a similar economic miracle. Moreover, it is known that Kim Jong Un himself has expressed interest in the Chinese and Vietnamese development paths, given their impressive results.[7] The place of the Second US-DPRK Summit, which took place in Hanoi, explains this.[8]

It seems quite natural that the DPRK would consider Vietnam as an exemplary model, given that Vietnam achieved a remarkable economic growth through market-oriented opening and reform policy over time without the dissolution of the Communist Party. Nonetheless, the DPRK presents a number of challenges and barriers that make it difficult for the country to emulate Vietnam as I have argued elsewhere.[9]

This is mainly due to the unique characteristics of the DPRK's political system, its nuclear weapons program, its ideology and system of governance, its geo-political dynamics, and above all, the division of the Korean nation between two Korean states, North and South. In this section, I further articulate the foundations for my belief that the DPRK would have to overcome completely different barriers in the process of opening and reform, which bear little resemblance to Vietnam.

First of all, unlike Vietnam, the significance of the North Korean leadership's courageous decision to denuclearize would mean shifting the state's development paradigm from rigid militarism to economic development. In this regard, rapid, sustained economic growth would be the only way to promptly regain the state's legitimacy—a rate of at least 10% average annual GDP growth will be necessary. Such a rate of growth exceeds those achieved by countries like South Korea, China, and Kazakhstan at the heights of their economic development.

Procrastinating development in North Korea would provoke acute social instability, which could further destabilize the inter-Korean relationship due to increasing economic disparity. Because of the income gap between the DPRK and the ROK—estimated at a magnitude of 45 to 50 times—masses of North Korean citizens may be tempted to defect, should Pyongyang introduce political opening without an adequate economic plan for sustainable growth. To mitigate these risks, tangible economic achievement within a short period of time is the only option for the DPRK to quickly enact the country's vision on long-term development.

Second, regarding the authority of the supreme ruler, the DPRK and Vietnam differ fundamentally. In North Korea, the legitimacy of the supreme leader in North Korea stems from the ruling system that Kim Il Sung designed to produce the fittest individual to realize and execute *Juche* ideology. The successor to become the next supreme ruler not only inherits absolute ruling power, but also the innate power to choose the next successor thereafter.[10] In other words, in the DPRK, all rules of authority are transferred to a single ruler.

In Vietnam, the executive system is organized according to the national constitution and establishes the authoritative system in control of political economic activities to be the communist regime. The power structure is collective and decentralized, composed by the Secretary, National Ruler, and the Prime Minister. The greatest figure of authority, the Secretary, is elected through competition within the central committee members. The national ruler assumes charge of the military and foreign affairs while the Prime Minister is in charge of overall internal affairs, including the national economy.

The discrepancy between the North Korean and Vietnamese ruling systems means that the change resulting from market-oriented reform and opening will have contrasting effects on the legitimacy of the authority of the supreme ruler. Market-oriented reform and opening would not only undermine the authority of the supreme leader but also harm the legitimacy of the system. In other words, this means that reform and opening, prerequisites for economic modernization, cannot occur without inflicting damage to the ruling system. For this reason, challenges of legitimacy represent an obstacle that only Kim Jong Un can resolve.

Third, the opening of a socialist regime inevitably brings forth some side effects as it exposes the fundamental flaws and distortions of the inefficient, prevailing system. North Korea would suffer far greater regime instability compared to Vietnam, as reform of the system will rely on the regime's ability to eliminate the underlying hypocrisies of the socialist system, which has deformed from its roots in traditional socialism, as explained in detail in Chap. 2. On the other hand, market-oriented opening is meant to achieve integration with the world economy, which depends heavily on foreign investment, influx of capital, the transfer of technology, business acumen, labor production and import-export systems. In the short term, reform and opening will destabilize the system—the privatization of state enterprises, for example, will inevitably produce bankruptcy. The process is a long and arduous one, and many hurdles to private firms will arise before they can gradually adjust and make a profit.

The same risks apply to opening for integration with the world market. The meaning and role of opening can be categorized as economic, which uses opening for economic development, but also as political, which would involve implementation of the basic human right of sharing information and knowledge. Even if we do not interpret "opening" as the basic right to information and knowledge through transparency with regard to political, economic, and public affairs, market-oriented opening will imply the likely disclosure of past human rights breaches and corruption to the public. However, without opening, there cannot be economic modernization through development and growth.

Fourth, in contrast with Vietnam, in order for the DPRK to accept denuclearization and achieve economic modernization, it must enter into a permanent peace treaty, enabling North-South cooperation. In short, North Korea cannot stop at the implementation of market-oriented reform; the regime must recognize that it will never successfully modernize if hostile North–South Korean relations persist. The North Korean military currently consists of 1.2 million soldiers and expends between 22% and 25% of the total national GDP on military-related purposes.[11] For the DPRK to denuclearize and achieve economic modernization, there must be a peace treaty between North and South Korea which rapidly resolves military hostility and reallocates high military expenditure to fostering of import-export industries instead, leading to the economic modernization of the DPRK. It is important to note that the two Koreas can agree upon a peace treaty, resolving the hostility between North Korea and the international community, only if the DPRK can successfully carry out reform of the system, changing the official ruling ideology.[12]

Thus, in comparing North Korea and Vietnam, the distinct differences, both positive and negative, that prevent the DPRK from mimicking Vietnam's model of economic transformation can be summarized as follows:

North Korea's unique challenges:

1. Kim Jong Un's hereditary succession: the constraints of carrying out *Juche* ideology must be resolved in order that legitimacy could stemming from popular support can be secured.
2. The division between North and South Korea: any faltering in the process of reform could undermine the survival of the regime, leading to absorption by South Korea.
3. The intense rivalry between North and South Korea: strong and sustained 10% GDP growth per annum is needed to neutralize the

destabilizing effects of transition and to close the GDP gap between the Koreas.

4. North Korea's low margin of error and lack of time: while Vietnam had the circumstances to experiment in trial and error, small missteps for the DRPK would instigate exodus and collapse.

North Korea's positional advantages:

1. They are surrounded by strong and dynamic economies: South Korea, Japan, China, and Russia will make vibrant partners.
2. Labor: the DPRK has is a well-trained, disciplined, and low cost labor force.
3. The value of the DPRK nuclear weapons: they can utilize in the exchange for a necessary development fund to finance the modernization drive.

The constraints and positional advantages North Korea possesses make learning lessons from Vietnam's opening and reform experience useful, but not a panacea that the DPRK can imitate. In undertaking economic modernization in North Korea, Kim Jong Un should take as much experience and information as he can, but the regime will need to blaze its own unique path.

3.3 Pertinent Lessons from the Experience of China

The various disparities between the respective restraints and advantages evidenced by North Korea and Vietnam limit the scope for its emulation as an ideal model for North Korean development. Ultimately, the country whose experience can offer the DPRK the most credible, practical lessons for economic reform is China. The policies of reform and opening put into place under Deng Xiaoping, which brought the country enormous prosperity and rapid development, that Kim Jong Un should emulate are summarized as follows.

3.3.1 Transcendence of Socialist Principles Through Political Reform Is Necessary

Unlike the final Soviet leader, Mikhail Gorbachev, whose attempts at implementing *glasnost'* and *perestroika* amounted to failed reform within the system, Deng Xiaoping understood that revitalizing the Chinese economy would demand addressing the issue of private ownership. In the economic sector, the people were ensured full autonomy in their economic activities, while dictatorship by the Communist Party was maintained in the political sector. As a result of this transformation, production means owned by the state were gradually privatized, thus ensuing autonomy for private corporations and resurrecting competition between companies, and the relinquishment of the state's monopoly on information regarding production and distribution changed the vertical structure of the centralized command economy into one of horizontal relationships instead.

The reason that Deng Xiaoping and the leadership under his regime were able to carry out market-oriented reform and opening can be attributed to the pragmatic compromise and flexibility they showed toward Mao Zedong's philosophies and legacy as the founder of the People's Republic of China. Deng and his followers deemed the Cultural Revolution that progressed under Mao to be a contradiction of the precepts of his own great works. Revealing his humanity through this fault prevented Mao from being deified as a god-like figure, though he remained a benevolent, great leader in the eyes of the people. Thus, the philosophies of Mao were prevented from expanding into absolute dogmatism—a crucial factor in China's development, as market-oriented reform must necessarily be preceded by political reform. During the process of China's economic reform and opening under the leadership of Deng Xiaoping, leading to the successful modernization of the Chinese economy, the active participation and support shown by key officials in the Communist Party and the military played a critical, leading role.

3.3.2 Ideological Indoctrination Must Be Eliminated

"It doesn't matter if the cat is black or white, so long as is catches mice."[13] This sentiment expressed by Deng is an allegory of his belief that if the socialist economic system has lost its relevance as a state development paradigm, then the yoke of ideological shackles restraining the economic system must be cast off and a new and reliable paradigm adopted. Another statement by Deng, that "[some party members] should get rich first," is a bold denouncement of the founding principles and ideas of the Communist Party. At the same time, it demonstrates the steadfast and unwavering determination Deng held in regard to the need for reform.

The purpose of ideological indoctrination is to instill loyalty to the ruling power and, through this, to promote social solidarity and control. The privatization of state corporations entirely defies ideological indoctrination, thus converting the party into one that must take the lead in ensuring that market-oriented reform is implemented successfully.

3.3.3 *Special Economic Zones (SEZs) Play a Critical Role*

The most significant lesson to be learned from the Chinese experience of opening and reform is their implementation of Special Economic Zones (SEZs), efforts which led the drive toward globalization of the Chinese economy. The Guangdong region, specifically, led exports under the auspices of the Chinese government and its radical foreign investment policy, thus producing an economic boom.

SEZs play a unique and critical role when any socialist nation seeks to modernize through market-oriented reform and opening. Most importantly, they offer the advantage of allowing a country to effectively control the various shocks and destabilizing effects that emanate from reform and opening, thus preserving the integrity of the socialist system. Alternatively, a sudden, comprehensive opening would destabilize the system and bury the socialist party. Instead, free-market systems can be introduced in controlled, isolated areas that have been identified for their comparative advantages.

Because economic development funds are initially scarce, there are many competing uses, but they should first be allocated to SEZs in order to construct infrastructure. As an essential element required for the globalization of the economy through integration with the global market, the establishment of a free market economy can first be implemented in select SEZs before expanding into other areas of the country.

Additionally, the enactment of foreign investment law within these zones attracts foreign capital necessary to augment growth through joint ventures and joint management schemes, the influx of foreign currency through exports, and the transferring of cutting-edge technology and efficient management knowledge into the country. Most importantly, though, SEZs offer the advantage of allowing a country to effectively control the various shocks and destabilizing effects that emanate from reform and opening, thus preserving the integrity of the socialist system. Alternatively, as sudden, comprehensive opening would destabilize the system and bury the socialist party.

3.3.4 *Attracting Foreign Investment Is Key*

As witnessed in the early stages of China's system reform and opening of its economy, SEZs established in the southern regions of China achieved remarkable success due to the various policies carried out by the government to attract foreign capital investment. In order to secure foreign capital through investment, Deng Xiaoping first had to transform hostile foreign relations with the international community into amicable, benign foreign policy. Combined with his implementation of radical foreign investment law, these measures paved the way for a stream of incoming investment from both foreign and overseas Chinese investors.

If SEZs are to attract and promote investment of foreign capital, legislation, in line with market economy principles and international norms, must be enacted and implemented. The legislation must include benefits and exemption plans for foreign investment, provisions for fruitage remittance, the right to exchange foreign currency into domestic currency at market rate, land lease, bankruptcy and liquidation, and an arbitration court to resolve disputes among enterprises.

3.3.5 *Legitimacy Has to Stem from Economic Reform*

While Deng Xiaoping managed to retain the stability and dominance of the socialist party throughout reform of the system and opening to the world economy, he recognized that the monolithic, god-like status of the party leader could not be reconciled with the new system. Instead, legitimacy had to be founded upon the dramatic improvement of the people's welfare and spectacular economic growth. Economic modernization and reform could not have taken place without the extraordinary leadership of Deng Xiaoping. This is seen through the transformation of China's economy, from the totalitarianism realized under the regime of Mao Zedong to authoritarianism following system reform under Deng Xiaoping.

The current situation in North Korea, of course, differs somewhat from the experience of China. North Korea has not only recognized Kim Il Sung as the founder of the greatest philosophical works in world history, namely *Juche* ideology, but also deified him as the only leader who could create a "heaven on earth," elevating Kim Il Sung to the status of an absolute being. This remains another hurdle for the North Korean leader to overcome to carry out market-oriented reforms, as the deification of Kim Il Sung continues to play a dominate role and serve as the cornerstone of the regime's legitimacy. However, it should be noted that when Kim Jong Un inherited the North Korean system, it had already distorted beyond recognition from its roots in *Juche* socialism, thus the constraints to implementing a paradigm shift in the nature of the regime have been somewhat alleviated.

If Kim Jong Un can become a "second Deng Xiaoping" by emulating the cases of China's reform, it will be a huge turning point in rewriting the country's history. If his genuine aspiration is the dramatically improve the welfare of the people, he must look to the challenges overcome by the great reformer of the Chinese economy. Without the audacity to face these obstacles, any attempt at modernization in North Korea will surely fail.

4 The North Korean Development Strategy: Strategic Approaches to Implementation of Market-Oriented Reform and Opening

The following section offers a strategic blueprint for the implementation of market-oriented reform and opening to achieve rapid development while controlling any destabilizing effects that could instigate domestic turmoil. The resulting failure or success of the blueprint depends conclusively on Kim Jong Un's ability to reform the North Korean system from one of extreme distortion to one rooted in market socialism.

4.1 Implementing a Viable Strategic Plan for Dynamic and Sustained Economic Development

Using the development fund provided by the stakeholders to transform into a market socialist system will entail that the economy is led by the ruling socialist party while allowing for private, joint and collective ventures to thrive. The relationship between the party and existing market activities must be redefined, making legal provision for the existence of a free labor market and free economic activity. Thus, the nature of the regime must fundamentally change: Kim Jong Un must transform his ruling system from totalitarianism to authoritarianism, preserving the party as the dominant actor through the process of privatization, institution building and legalization of free market activity.

4.2 *The Goal of Economic Modernization and the Meaning of 10% Annual Growth*

As the DPRK launches the drive for economic modernization and transforms into a system of market socialism, the target annual GDP growth rate will become relevant. Determining the optimum GDP target is essential to its survival and the foundation of sustained prosperity for the economy: The optimum minimum average GDP growth rate per annum is 10% over 10 years, the reasons for which are explained below.

1. *The size of the economic development fund to be contributed by the five stakeholders*
   The amount of funds contributed to North Korea's reform and opening is directly linked to the survival and legitimacy of Kim Jong Un. Therefore, the target average minimum GDP growth rate per annum must be sufficiently large to rationalize the provision of a large development fund.
2. *Objective justification for accepting denuclearization*
   Not only would a sustained 10% GDP growth be phenomenal for North Korea, but it would also be historic on the world stage. Such robust economic growth would supply a new source of legitimacy for Kim Jong Un as he leads his country towards a monumental achievement. This is essential because Kim Jong-un will no longer be able to draw power and the credibility to lead from his heritage nor from his achievement of nuclear capabilities; instead, he will need the mandate of the people.
3. *Justification of the radical revision of the official guiding ideology of the state*
   Thanks to rapid and sustained economic growth, the North Korean people will experience real, radical improvement of their wellbeing, moving beyond the tenets of *Juche* ideology to give their genuine popular support to Kim Jong Un. This will enable him to relieve the burden of carrying out *Juche* ideology, leaving behind the distorted socialist system to embrace transformation into an efficient, market socialist economy.
4. *Infrastructure construction as a prerequisite for economic modernization*
   As new infrastructure and investments are built and developed, it will bring a vivid enhancement to the North Korean people's welfare

at a rapid speed. As the populace see their standards of living improve, it will inspire hope that will make the opportunities in North Korea become more attractive than in Seoul or elsewhere. If economic growth is sluggish, some will be tempted to desert. While they must be free to, expeditious growth would neutralize these concerns.

5. *Disintegration of external and internal control mechanisms, to be replaced by job security*

   Throughout the process of privatization during opening and reform, the state labor market will be released to integrate with the private sector. The average minimum GDP growth rate per annum must be sufficiently impressive to ensure that former state workers enjoy job security through the creation of gainful employment in newly-privatized enterprises. This security, thus, functions to replace the current apparatuses of external and internal control, including the rationing system, control of unauthorized information and punishment.

6. *Sufficiently robust economic growth to contain destabilizing effects of opening and reform*

   During a transition from a socialist system to a market economy, there is massive instability. In order to effectively contain ill-effects during transition, North Korea needs new economic vitality, but an average minimum GDP growth rate that is lower than 10% will not provide sufficient impetus to override the acute volatility during transition.

7. *Reducing the income gap between North and South Korea*

   If the enormous disparity between wealth and everyday living standards in the North and the South remains stark, genuine economic reform and opening will never succeed. North Koreans will be compelled across the border to the South in search of opportunity and well-being. Therefore, the average minimum GDP growth rate per annum must be so robust that citizens will pursue opportunities in their own rapidly developing economy.

8. *Independently sustaining rapid economic growth after the expiration of the agreement*

The North Korean economy must be assured the provision of a development fund for 10 years in order to pave the road for their economic modernization. After the conclusion of the agreement, however, that must no longer rely on external financial help to achieve their sustained economic growth. Thus, their average minimum GDP growth per annum for the first 10 years must lay a firm foundation for continued spectacular growth.

4.3 *The $300 Billion Economic Development Fund*

Should North Korea accept complete, verifiable and irreversible denuclearization (CVID), the regime will require rapid economic transition through the quick establishment of a foundation for modernization, accomplished through the dynamic annual economic growth of 10% per annum, as explained above. In order to achieve such rapid growth, North Korea must secure at least $30 billion annually over an initial period of 10 years, for a total of $300 billion. This annual $30 billion development fund is equivalent to North Korea's annual gross national product (GDP), 2% of South Korea's GNP (gross national product), and 70% of South Korea's total military expenditure.

First of all, if North Korea carries out market-oriented reform followed by opening with friendly foreign policy, the regime will face serious risk of the disintegration of its internal systems of bureaucratic control, as well as external risks due to the sudden creation of a security vacuum. This is due to the fact that market-oriented system reform may result in the disintegration of the bureaucratic function of oppressive control (e.g. ideology, culture, and rationing system). Moreover, the shift in foreign policy from hostile to friendly could cause a loss of external control—the strategy of viewing neighboring countries as enemies and using brinkmanship as a negotiation tool, which have long functioned as justification for the military first policy and as a means of consolidating the solidarity of the people. In order to prevent the security vacuum both internally and externally, development funds should be available to stabilize the society.

Secondly, the development fund should be used to ensure that the state enterprises are privatized, state employees are integrated into the labor force, jobs are created, infrastructure is developed and a social security system is established to improve the people's welfare. Before the reduction of military forces and release of laborer employed by the state can cause societal instability, the work force should be quickly absorbed by private companies. For example, infrastructure construction can have a positive effect on social stability by providing jobs for the unemployed and increasing their income. If one million people were hired to construct roads, railways, electricity, water infrastructure, ports, airports and irrigation projects, the average annual wage per person would convert to $1400, resulting in a total of $1.4 billion in primary income. The extra income derived from per capita marginal propensity to consume would be several times this $1.4 billion figure.

Thirdly, in order to attract foreign capital for economic modernization, investment must first be made for infrastructure construction. Construction and repair of electric power plants, water infrastructure, ports, roads, railways, telecommunications and airport infrastructure require a large sum of immediately-available funds. Financing for infrastructure construction cannot be entirely dependent on international financial institutions. One important reason is that the process of approving loans is extremely complicated and would take a very long time.

Fourthly, in order to ensure market-oriented reform and openness is linked effectively to economic modernization, skilled personnel, trained in market conditions, are needed to lead the related sectors. Among them are researchers, government officials, bankers and economic experts who will map out economic plans, including entrepreneurs who can operate and manage private companies. The estimated minimum cost per person to receive training abroad for a period one year is approximately $50,000, thus the cost to send 10,000 workers for this period would total at $500 million.

Fifthly, the economic development fund must be allocated to the establishment of critical institutions. These include a ministry of finance, central banking system, internal revenue services, bureau of statistics and systems for social security and education.

Based on the above-explained justifications, North Korea will need, at minimum, $30 billion annually for the coming decade, and a clear blueprint for economic reform must be sufficiently discussed in parallel with negotiations for denuclearization.

4.4 *Who Should Be the Main Contributor to North Korea's Economic Development?*

The economic development fund, which will be provided as a counterweight to North Korea's nuclear dismantlement, should be mobilized by all five stakeholder countries—South Korea, China, Japan, Russia and the United States. The main justification for this is that the North's denuclearization is in line with the strategic interests of those countries. However, the primary contributor country of the fast track economic development fund should be, first and foremost, South Korea.

South Korea is the country that will benefit most from the North's economic leap forward. If the North's economic development fund is injected into infrastructure construction, the bulk of the investment will return to the income of South Korean companies involved in infrastructure construction. It costs about $3 billion to modernize port facilities and $6 billion to build a medium-sized thermal power plant. Most of the investment returns to the income of South Korean companies involved in the various construction projects. Additionally, if the North succeeds in remarkable dynamic and sustained economic growth, the South can enjoy synergy towards shared growth, freeing itself from the low-growth swamp.

For the stability of the peninsula and the region, the two Koreas must be able to narrow the income gap as much as possible. This huge economic disparity is an inevitable obstacle to cooperation and integration, even causing inter-Korean conflict. By supporting the North's remarkable sustained economic growth, the two Koreas can open the way for peace and stability on the peninsula through gradual economic integration as a single nation, thus making the DPRK a viable state, a reliable neighbor and partner of the dynamic region of East Asia.

If efforts to modernize the economy through the denuclearization of North Korea lead to catastrophe, South Korea will be the nation to suffer the most. For example, if 10% of the North Korean population, or 2.5 million, defected to the South due to economic difficulties and calamity, the social costs incurred by them alone are estimated to exceed $25 billion a year.

Finally, in order to enable future prospects of reunification, the DPRK must achieve spectacular growth as to avoid any risk of political absorption. This should be an objective for the South as well: even if both Korean states can benefit from unification in the distant future, it is important to specify that in the short and medium term, they ought to focus solely on the North's economic reconstruction and stability, making it clear that neither Korean state (North or South) will seek political integration before a solid and durable economic pattern of growth is established by Pyongyang. To this end, one of the first steps for both Koreas in implementing the blueprint proposed in this volume is to drastically reduce their respective military expenditures, redirecting their resources to infrastructure building for economic development.

4.5 Groundwork for Economic Integration with the World Economy

If North Korea Chairman were to embrace the modernization of North Korea's economy through the successful implementation of the following measures, the result would produce sustained economic development at a rate unprecedented in world history. Each of the elements described below are closely interconnected and function together to control the shocks involved in opening and reform.

4.5.1 Privatization

First, the DPRK must privatize state-owned corporations to reduce the state sector and gradually expand a market economy through participation from the private sector. According to recent reports, production from the unofficial sector already accounts for more than half of the DPRK's gross national product (GNP). Nurturing and developing this unofficial sector into a market economy will require the enactment of laws that allow for a wide variety of forms of private corporations to be founded and operated, namely state- and privately-owned corporations, joint ventures between the state and private entities, joint stock companies, and entrusted management. It will also be necessary to privatize state-owned corporations and reallocate the facilities and land owned by these companies to the private sector.

Legal provisions must be established to allow private corporations to freely hire the workers laid off due to this privatization of state corporations after they are allowed to join the free labor market. It that must be kept in mind is that such market-oriented reform will first and foremost require political reform.

Second, a set of measures must be performed to globalize the economy through a reasonable form of economic opening. The basic requirement for the globalization of the DPRK's economy will be to liberalize economic activities. In other words, it will be necessary to eliminate all bureaucratic controlling measures that block integration with the global economy.

The following measures can serve as the means to promote the globalization of the DPRK's economy:

1. Newly-established private corporations should be legally and systematically allowed to establish joint ventures or engage in joint management and/or consignment production schemes with foreign

corporations in order to earn foreign currency, stimulate employment, and promote the transfer of the latest technology and management knowledge.

2. Legislation must be enacted and put into effect to establish a free labor market and allow joint ventures and private corporations to pay competitive wages and hire/dismiss workers within this free labor market.
3. All bureaucratic controlling measures that impede activities within the market economy should be withdrawn. More specifically, the following measures should be taken:
   - The so-called "mosquito net" of measures taken by the regime to prevent ideological poisoning and contamination must be abolished;
   - Laborers must be guaranteed their freedom of relocation and movement;
   - Corporations and their managers/employees must be guaranteed free communication via email, telephones, fax, etc.;
   - The managers of foreign corporations must be legally guaranteed the freedom to perform field training and visit their contractors within the nation; and
   - Personnel affiliated with foreign and domestic corporations must be guaranteed free travel across the border.
4. A commercial code in accordance with the general principles of a market economy and international norms must be enacted and put into effect. This commercial code should include provisions for the following items:

   - Remittances from foreign corporations;
   - Application of a single exchange rate;
   - Protection of property rights;
   - Establishment, bankruptcy, and liquidation of corporations;
   - Mediation and resolution of disputes at an international arbitration court;
   - Leasing of land; and
   - Tax benefits in exchange for investment by foreign corporations.

Ultimately, privatization is the backbone of economic reform and opening. Therefore, the success or failure of the economic modernization of the DPRK depends upon the extent to which privatization can be successfully implemented.

4.5.2 *Introduction of an Expert Committee*

The main role of the expert committee will be to establish, oversee, and supervise policies for system reform aimed at modernizing the economy and expediting GDP growth to the target 10% annually. As we can see from Kazakhstan's experience, establishing an expert committee that is directly chaired and led by the president of the country not only contributed greatly to the successful implementation of reform and modernization, it also played a crucial role in the nation's remarkable growth into a leading Central Asian country.

As the DPRK lacks experts with experience in the process of system reform and economic modernization and deep knowledge of market economies, the process of reform, centered on the privatization of state corporations, will be difficult and painful. Nonetheless, if the DPRK is to minimize the trials and errors occurring throughout this process, and modernize its economy at a rapid pace and relatively low cost, it will be imperative to establish an expert committee. The expert committee should be comprised of foreign experts possessing knowledge and experience in system reform and opening, working together with domestic experts as their counterparts.

Considering the enormous authority and responsibility associated with operating the expert committee, this advisory body should be chaired by the highest leader of the country because the act of reform is not only an economic issue but also a political one. The process will involve immense obstacles and will be an arduous challenge, but only the leadership is equipped to overcome them. As vice chairmen, one foreign and one domestic expert should be appointed.

The primary duties of the expert committee will include drafting comprehensive policy recommendations to privatize state-owned corporations, designing and founding state institutions, constructing new infrastructure, identifying leading sectors to foster, promoting agriculture, selecting and ensuring the operation of special economic zones, administering social security systems, and developing human resources. All policy recommendations will have to weigh the costs, time requirement, and political ramifications of each respective initiative, and to initiate implementation, Chairman Kim Jong Un will have to provide his final approval.

4.5.3 *Support from Core Party and Military Officials*

The act of introducing opening and reform in North Korea will demand incredible dedication on the part of Kim Jong Un, necessitating his unyielding commitment to the execution of a blueprint for system reform and modernization. During the process of China's economic reform and opening under the leadership of Deng Xiaoping, leading to the successful modernization of the Chinese economy, the active participation and support shown by key officials in the Communist Party and the military played a critical role.

Market-oriented system reform and opening cannot succeed without political reform. As a prerequisite, system reform demands a political structure that will enable opening of the economy to be carried out. Deng Xiaoping employed both persuasion and pressure as necessary to convince core officials to take an active lead in implementing the reform process.

"If we don't change, we are at a dead end! Whoever doesn't reform will have to step down!"—Deng Xiaoping, 1992

The above sentiment by Deng speaks both to the determination he possessed toward reform and opening and to the importance of party and military officials' active participation and support of this process. Ensuring that core party and military officials took an active part in the reform and opening process had the effect of curtailing opposition from these sectors, which if left unchecked could have caused the process to run aground. In order for economic reform and opening to proceed unfalteringly it must be led by core party and military officials.

4.5.4 *Establishment of Special Economic Zones (SEZs)*

As discussed in great detail in Part 4 of this chapter, the Chinese experience demonstrates that Special Economic Zones (SEZs) play an integral and unique role in the opening and reform of a socialist system. With these strategic advantages in mind, in North Korea, three or four SEZs should be initially selected for focused development of a market economy, after which other areas can be identified for similar treatment. This isolated implementation of market-oriented reform guarantees that the process of opening will not threaten the safety or stability of the regime. It will be necessary to first establish a sufficient quality of infrastructure in SEZs if they are to achieve their intended purpose and role. The construction of infrastructure requires a massive amount of funds and long periods of time, making it difficult to carry out all at once. This is why investments to construct and improve infrastructure should first be focused in SEZs.

For an SEZ to perform its intended role properly, the following measures and conditions must be taken/satisfied:

1. Investment must be made to improve and establish infrastructure (e.g. electricity, telecommunication, railroads, roads and airports). Without such initiatives, foreign entrepreneurs will not be interested in investing in the country.
2. Consideration must be given to the geographic and strategic advantages presented by the region when selecting the location for SEZs. In light of the need to develop infrastructure and establish these regions as free market economies, it would be pragmatic to initially establish four SEZs in the initial stages, and then establish additional SEZs at a later point.
3. Export industries and other sectors possessing comparative advantages should be given priority in SEZs.
4. The level of control exerted by an inefficient and centralized bureaucracy must be eased, and the authority and responsibility required to operate and manage these special zones must be delegated to local governments.
5. Authority must be granted for private enterprises and joint stock companies to divide ownership into half-state and half-private entities to freely participate in economic activities.
6. Bureaucratic control aimed at suppressing so-called "ideological pollution" must be withdrawn. Within the system of joint ventures and consignment processing, field training and travel must be allowed to take place freely. Communications must be ensured between companies in a free manner.
7. A free labor market must be created, and joint ventures and private enterprises must be guaranteed the right to issue competitive pay to their workers according to demand and supply in the labor market, and to freely hire and terminate workers.
8. Legislation for special economic zones must be enacted and implemented. If the SEZs are to attract and promote investment of foreign capital, the laws that govern them must be in line with market economy principles and international norms. The legislation must include benefits and exemption plans for foreign investment, comprehensive trade policies guided by WTO standards, most-favored nation provisions, protection from expropriation, provisions for remittances, the right to exchange foreign currency into domestic currency at market rate, land lease laws, bankruptcy and liquidation regulations, and arbitration courts that abide by the New York Arbitration Convention.

4.5.5 *Infrastructure Development*

The current deficient state of infrastructure within the DPRK would make sustained and high economic growth impossible. The state of the DPRK's infrastructure can be summarized as follows:

1. The DPRK has roughly 724 kilometers of paved roads, less than 1% of the total length of paved roads in South Korea, and the roads that are currently available are in poor condition. To achieve spectacular economic growth, roads must be repaired and constructed to ensure the flow of goods and merchandise.
2. The total electric output capacity of the DPRK amounts to 13 billion kilowatt hours (kWh), or one-fortieth (1/40) of South Korea's. This is drastically short of the output needed for rapid development, and the deteriorated state of existing generators and network stations leads to frequent blackouts.
3. The DPRK possesses roughly 6000 kilometers in railroads. While the total length of its railroads exceeds that within South Korea (3668 kilometers), a lack of investment in improvement and maintenance has left the railroads in a poor state.
4. The DPRK has 17 ports, the seven main ports being Sonbong, Hungnam, Nampo, Songlim, Seongbong, Wonsan, and Haeju. Port facilities are in poor repair and maintain a severely limited capacity for logistic processing.
5. There are approximately 78 airports in the DPRK. The outdated control towers and deteriorated runways at these airports will require investment to repair and modernize these facilities.
6. The existing communications infrastructure must be repaired and expanded to allow for nationwide connection and development. Investment in the construction of new infrastructure plays an important political and economic role, and it must be undertaken immediately as a prerequisite to modernization, as projects such as road or port building can demand upwards of 3–5 years to complete.

The strategic plan to modernize the DPRK's economy is centered on system reform and the liberalization of its economy and includes the mobilization of 2 million workers annually, to be utilized in various infrastructure construction projects. Selecting workers from those who lost jobs at privatized national corporations, or military personnel discharged due to cuts in the military expenditure, will ensure job security and increase income.

The creation of jobs and increase in income will have a stabilizing effect on the regime by replacing the role hitherto performed by such bureaucratic control systems as the public distribution system. Investment to construct new infrastructure also contributes to economic growth in proportion to the growing gross domestic product (GDP). Payment of annual wages for each laborer should total at $1000, for a total of $2 billion necessary to employ 2 million laborers. While the initial income rise after payment of these wages is 2 billion dollars, when factoring in the estimated marginal propensity to consume at 80% (0.8), the subsequent multiplier effect will induce a further cumulative income five times the original investment, approximately $10 billion

4.5.6 *Identification and Fostering of Leading Sectors*

In order to stimulate rapid economic growth, it will be necessary for the DPRK to identify and foster leading sectors—those that can be identified for their comparative advantages and most effectively optimize economic development funds, the given labor force and resources at hand. The following areas can act as such leading industrial sectors for North Korea's economic development:

1. *Labor-intensive industries*

   The DPRK is equipped with a very large, highly-skilled, and industrious labor force. Labor-intensive industries, such as construction, mining, fishing, and textiles will allow the DPRK to utilize its remarkably large workforce at a low cost and offer services and products at competitive prices. These industries have a synergy effect on the economy and will become great engines of growth, having further-reaching positive impacts, as well. For example, the construction of apartments, houses, office buildings, hotels, and other civil engineering projects will have a positive impact on the gross national product.
2. *Real estate*

   Once it becomes possible for individuals to own their own apartments and industrial buildings, the real estate sector will contribute to the gross national product and, in turn, boost other industries. Real estate is essentially a backbone of economic development as it generates a variety of income sources, thus creating a synergy effect.

3. *Tourism*

   North Korea is blessed with abundant tourism resources, which are in turn linked to the hotel and transportation industries (railroad, airport, seaport, roads). Therefore if North Korea is to promote its tourism industry, it will first have to construct the infrastructure facilities necessary for these industries. Promoting tourism can make a major contribution to North Korea's gross national product.

4. *Logistics*

   North Korea is situated in a geopolitically important location. Once the railroad that connects Shinuiju and Busan is restored and Rajin, Sonbong, Wonsan are connected by railroad as well, the transportation of goods between the two Koreas will generate massive profits. The roads and railroads connecting Korea and China, Russia, Europe, and the Middle East will not only play an important role in the economic development of North Asia but also serve as an important source of revenue for North Korea.

4.5.7 Monetary and Fiscal Policy

In a market economy, monetary and fiscal policy is one of the most important instruments to a successful economic opening policy. The introduction of monetary policy boosts and stabilizes the economy through the establishment of money supply policy, interest rate control and regulation of commercial banks. Fiscal policy, meanwhile, is crucial because it sets tax policy and government expenditure, which should be largely allocated to the construction of roads and other infrastructure crucial to development.

Foreign currencies are essential to keep prices stable. In order for North Korea to achieve market-oriented reform and opening to establish a basis for economic modernization, it must be able to maintain price stability that directly affects the people's overall well-being. To ensure price stability, the government must maintain and operate a certain level of foreign currency reserves. Like all existing socialist countries, North Korea has suffered severe inflation. Foreign exchange reserves, which are required to maintain price stability and are often referred to as sovereign funds, are already undergoing a trade deficit due to a continued slowdown in exports, as pointed out above.

It should be noted that foreign reserves are vital to ensure the stability of the economy. Thus, in order for North Korea to succeed in modernizing its economy, it must be able to secure the optimal amount of economic development funds from foreign countries in exchange for abandonment of weapons of mass destruction, including nuclear weapons. The funds are used as a means of curbing inflation due to monetary expansion caused by the employment of millions of workers and the settlement of their wages in won, which will be mobilized to build infrastructure that is essential for economic modernization.

Let's analyze the effect of fluctuation of foreign reserves on price stability. Rice prices and exchange rates in the North Korean market are determined by the demand and supply of rice and foreign currencies in the market.[14] The North Korean authorities are known to determine market rice prices based on the cost of rice, market demand and supply, international market prices and exchange rate quotes, and determine the exchange rate of the US dollar, based on the price of rice.[15] Therefore, the causes of inflation can be largely explained in four ways.

1. Inflation depends on the fluctuation of rice supply, and the supply of rice depends on rice production and imports.
2. Fluctuations are caused by increases in the amount of local currency.
3. Fluctuations in exchange rates are also caused by the demand and supply of foreign currencies. For example, if exports are reduced due to a slowdown in exports, or political instability leads to an increase in demand for dollars, it will cause a rise in the exchange rate, which will, in turn, lead to an increase in rice prices.
4. An increase in imports of consumer goods, including commodities, due to fluctuations in exports will lead to fluctuations in commodity and consumer prices. For example, slowing exports lead to a decrease in imports of consumer goods, including commodities, leading to an increase in commodity prices.

The explanations above give us the message that government authorities cannot stabilize prices without adequate foreign currency and efficient operation. Regarding the calculation of the appropriate foreign currency reserves, South Korea, for example, has a foreign currency of US $403.6 billion,[16] equivalent to 24.6% of the total national income of US $1.6 trillion, as of 2018. Kazakhstan, as another example, maintains 12.5% of its total national income of US $946.2 billion.[17] If North Korea's total national income is estimated at US $35 billion, it means that it must maintain at least US $7 billion in foreign reserves, worth 20% of the total national income.

Another reason for the need for an economic development fund consisting of foreign currencies is to create and support employment for the people who will be released in the process of the privatization of state enterprises, the reduction of military personnel, and the restructuring of the military industry.

In order to stabilize the value of the currency, the wages of the workers hired for the construction of infrastructure must be paid out in national currency, namely North Korean won. Once the money is spent, it must be retired from the economy by appropriating foreign reserves to importers who will import goods like food, technology, raw materials and other wares.

4.5.8 *Institution Building*

Institution building must be executed through the founding of a centralized bank, a ministry of finance, internal revenue services, bureau of statistics and systems for social security and education.

It will be necessary to establish a centralized bank and ministry of finance in order to unify the monetary system and implement macroeconomic policies. In its present state, the coupled effects of institutional privilege and competition amongst bureaucratic organizations, those that engage in foreign trade and maintain foreign currency reserves, prevent dollarization and stabilize the economy through unified economic policies. By establishing a centralized bank and a ministry of finance, the government will be capable of setting fiscal goals, regulating trade, maintaining foreign currency reserves, and implementing large-scale economic policies to sustain and support the country's rapid economic transition. Additionally, the business of loan lending, currently under the control of the *Donju* social class, must be officially transferred to full-fledged commercial banks, along with savings accounts, to eradicate corruption.

Social security systems will have a direct impact on the social and political stability of North Korea by providing welfare measures for disabled people, pension beneficiaries, the economically underprivileged, and workers who have lost their jobs due to the privatization of state corporations. Such social security systems will mitigate unrest, improve economic livelihood, and help maintain political stability.

There is a complete lack of reliable statistical information in North Korea, such as a census or data regarding per capita income. In order to establish a viable economy, a bureau of statistic must be founded to provide this crucial information.

To equip the population with the knowledge and resources necessary to carry out radical reform and opening of their centralized economy, it will be paramount that the rising generation of North Koreans are educated according to international standards of excellence in business, economics, information technology, and public administration. Therefore, the establishment of an education system, designed to prepare students for Western-style higher education, must be prioritized to meet the needs of the new market economy.

4.5.9 Development of Human Resources

Ultimately, the modernization of a nation's economy is not achieved by natural resources or a corporate organization; it is achieved by people. China and Kazakhstan demonstrated that competent individuals who have received excellent training and education at Western-style universities not only play an important role during the process of economic reform and opening, they serve as the driving force that enables a nation to achieve remarkable economic development.

In order to modernize the nation's economy, it will be necessary to foster and produce competent individuals who can operate and manage newly founded private enterprises, establish reasonable economic policies, and execute national-level tasks in an efficient manner. The pace at which economic modernization is achieved depends on how fast a nation can generate individuals who have been superbly trained and educated at Western-style universities.

As a measure to foster the competent experts and talent that North Korea will need, the following three proposals should be considered:

1. A minimum of 10,000 qualified and talented individuals should be sent overseas to study abroad at Western universities. This will require an annual budget of approximately 400 million dollars, which should be borne by the state.
2. A Western-style university should be founded within the nation, thus allowing experts to be trained domestically, as well. As Kazakhstan's experience has shown, establishing a Western-style university to foster young talent is drastically cheaper than sending students overseas for higher education, and can produce comparable results.

3. Seminars and symposiums should be hosted to invite foreign experts to share their knowledge on modern management and the latest technology, and joint venture companies should work to share managerial know-how and technology through field training.

4.5.10 Revitalization of the Agricultural Sector

There is a tendency for economists to overlook the important role played by the agricultural industry throughout the process of system reform and economic modernization. The contributions of the agricultural sector to this process can be summarized as follows:

1. The provision of ample food not only improves the lives of laborers, but the general public, and has a direct impact on the quality of labor, as well. It is essential to increasing food production and supply, and promoting productivity in the agricultural industry sector allows the state to ensure an adequate food supply for laborers and the general population.
2. The agricultural industry bears a mutual and complementary relationship with the industrial sector. An increase in agricultural productivity leads to better income for farming households, and this increase in income facilitates demand for fertilizer, pesticide, agricultural equipment and other necessities produced by the industrial sector. In turn, growth and development in the industrial sector enables fertilizer, pesticide, agricultural equipment, etc. to be produced and supplied on time and in sufficient quantities.
3. The labor force saved through an increase in agricultural productivity, i.e. the idle manpower no longer needed in the agricultural sector, can be transferred to the industrial sector to provide labor needed there. A total of 4.75 million DPRK citizens, or approximately 23.4% of the working population, are employed in the agricultural industry. The DPRK's agricultural productivity is estimated at 60% to 70% of South Korea and other advanced economies.

The agricultural industry plays an important role during the process of reform and economic modernization. Advances in the agricultural sector can be realized not only with relatively small investment, but also at a more rapid pace when compared with the industrial sector and other industries.

Due to an expansion of policies to place residents in charge of their own plots and to vitalize grassroots markets, food supply in the DPRK has visibly improved. The current system groups three to five residents into a single unit in charge of a specific farming plot. Residents submit to the state 50% to 70% of the grain produced from the plot as public tax, but are granted the authority to dispose of the remaining grain at the market as they please. In spite of the success of this system, the DPRK's agricultural productivity remains well below that of Western nations.

4.6 *The Terms of the Deal*

In order to realize North Korea's denuclearization through the framework of the six-party talks, the terms of agreement that the five parties will jointly present to the North must be in the form a comprehensive package deal. Complete, verifiable, and irreversible denuclearization (CVID) of North Korea will require the active participation and unyielding commitment of all stakeholder nations (the U.S., South Korea, China, Japan, and Russia) to effectively utilize all sticks and carrots at hand, as explored in great detail in Part 2 of this chapter.

The carrots offered by the stakeholder nations must guarantee a credible opportunity for regime survival without nuclear weapons—economic modernization in exchange for dismantlement of the nuclear program. Likewise, the stakeholders' sticks must exert collective pressure in the form of economic sanctions and military coercion so unrelenting that regime change would certainly ensue should Chairman Kim reject the offer or fail to uphold the terms of agreement.

In order to establish peace and stability on the Korean Peninsula through North Korea's denuclearization and open the way for common economic prosperity between the two Koreas, the package deal blueprint must include stipulations that North Korea will:

1. Dismantle all weapons of mass destruction,
2. Accept unlimited International Atomic Energy Agency (IAEA) inspections; and
3. Introduce a market system to rapidly modernize its economy.

Meanwhile, the five parties should contribute the withdrawal of all sanctions and pressure, diplomatic ties between North Korea and the U.S., diplomatic ties between North Korea and Japan, the establishment of a peace treaty between South Korea and North Korea and contribution of economic development funds under the recognition of two separate systems on the Korean Peninsula. This is why the five-party countries must create a comprehensive package deal to successfully realize the North's denuclearization and achieve economic prosperity based on peace and stability.

In the past, the U.S. has employed a piecemeal approach to negotiating with North Korea, whereby the regime would offer portions of its nuclear arsenal and, upon verification, the U.S. would reciprocate. A gradual, trade-off approach to dealings with Kim Jong Un, however, is doomed to fail: North Korean weapons of mass destruction extend beyond nuclear capabilities to an arsenal of chemical and other offensive weapons. Most importantly, though, as this section has already discussed, neither the U.S. nor any other single stakeholder nation possesses all of the "sticks" and "carrots" necessary to induce the total disarmament of the DPRK.

This is why any proposal for denuclearization, formulated on the basis of a shared policy between all five of the stakeholder nations, must be comprehensive in nature. It must provide North Korea with a genuine chance at achieving economic modernization— an offer that he could not possibly refuse—and it must be put forward in the form of a one-off deal for economic modernization and prosperity that demands immediate action; no trade-offs involved.

5 Conclusion

In order to persuade Kim Jong Un that denuclearization holds a genuine chance for survival through economic reform and modernization, he must be convinced that the benefits of acceptance considerably outweigh the costs of retaining nuclear weapons. With the unyielding support of all five of the stakeholder nations, with the countries that stand to gain the most from the DPRK's development—South Korea and China—providing sizable contributions to an economic development fund, an enticing package deal can be put forward.

Such a deal, however, must be more than transactional in scope—it must also demand transformation of the very nature of the regime. The North Korean system is more than archaic or inefficient; it has distorted so radically from its socialist origins that it is nearly unrecognizable. If any plan for economic reform and opening is to be put into place, it must first ensure that the fundamentally-flawed system is replaced entirely by one based upon market principles, as well as that the nation is opened for integration with the world economy and hostile approaches to foreign policy are abandoned in favor of amicable relations.

With an economic fund in place, a sufficiently spectacular development goal must be instituted—a minimum annual GDP growth rate of 10% over a 10-year period. This figure is important both practically and symbolically, as such growth will gradually decrease the enormous gap between the North and the South, cementing Kim Jong Un's legitimacy as leader and justifying his choice to dismantle the nuclear weapons program. In order to ensure the achievement of this goal, a tangible, cohesive blueprint must be formulated, drawing on the lessons learned from the experiences of other formerly socialist economies while acknowledging the unique situation of North Korea. Such a blueprint must entail the establishment of infrastructure, special economic zones, an expert committee, trade facilities, financial institutions, banking, legal reforms, human resource development and employment for state laborers and military personnel, among other measures.

I have little doubt that, if Chairman Kim decides firmly to accept denuclearization and proceed with policies of reform and opening, with the support and cooperation of the five stakeholder countries, the DPRK has enormous potential to achieve historically-unprecedented and miraculous economic growth.

Notes

1. Fifield, Anna. 2019. The Great Successor: The Divinely Perfect Destiny of Brilliant Comrade Kim Jong Un. New York: Public Affairs. p. 276.
2. Silberstein, Benjamin Katzeff. 2019. "Kim Jong-un's speech at the SPA in April 2019." *North Korean Economy Watch*. Retrieved from https://www.nkeconwatch.com/2019/04/14/kim-jong-uns-speech-at-the-spa-in-april-2019/.
3. Kim, Jack. 2019. "North Korea's Kim: I don't want my children to bear burden of nuclear arms—report." *Reuters*. Retrieved from https://www.reuters.com/article/us-northkorea-usa-kim/north-koreas-kim-i-dont-want-my-children-to-bear-burden-of-nuclear-arms-report-idUSKCN1QC0CZ.
4. Fifield, Anna. 2019. *The Great Successor: The Divinely Perfect Destiny of Brilliant Comrade Kim Jong Un*. New York: Public Affairs. p. 267.
5. Bang, Chan Young. 1995. *The Democratic People's Republic of Korea at a crossroad, Park Young-sa*. Seoul: Bak Young Sa. pp. 181–242.

6. Stradiotto, Guo. 2007. "The Nature and Direction of Economic Reform in North Korea." *Political Studies* 55: 754–778.
7. Delury, John. 2018. "Kim Jong-un Has a Dream. The U.S. Should Help Him Realize It." *The New York Times.* Retrieved from https://www.nytimes.com/2018/09/21/opinion/kim-jong-un-moon-economic-development-north-korea-denuclearization.html.
8. Beech, Hannah. 2019. "Vietnam Summit Hosts Offer North Korea a Model: Cozy Up to the U.S." *New York Times.* Retrieved from https://www.nytimes.com/2019/02/26/world/asia/trump-kim-vietnam-summit-north-korea-relations.html.
9. See, for example, Bang, Chan Young. 2018. "Why North Korea Can't Follow in Vietnam's Footsteps." *The Diplomat.* Retrieved from https://thediplomat.com/2018/07/why-north-korea-cant-follow-in-vietnams-footsteps/.
10. Park, Yong-soo. 2009. "The Political Economy of Economic Reform in North Korea." *Australian Journal of International Affairs* 63 (4): 529–549.
11. Yonhap News. 2016. "N. Korea ranks No. 1 for military spending relative to GDP: State Department report." Retrieved from en.yna.co.kr/view/AEN20161223000200315.
12. KINU. 2017. *Analysis of 2017 North Korea's New Year's Day Speech and Prospect for its Internal and External Policy.*
13. Hung, Li. 1977. *China's Political Situation and the Power Struggle in Peking.*
14. Kim, Suk-Jin & Yang, Moon-Soo. 2015. *The Growth of the Informal Economy in North Korea*. Seoul: KINU.
15. Jung hoon, L. 2014. *North Korea's Market Price and Inflation-Related Issues.* Seoul: Hanul. pp. 230–231.
16. Bank of Korea. 2018. *Foreign Exchange Reserves.*
17. Agency of Statistics of the Republic of Kazakhstan. 2018. GDP and holding foreign currency Kazakhstan.

Bibliography

Abott, Felix. 2015. *Pyongyang capitalism (seven years of life in Pyongyang by a Swiss businessman) [Pyeongyangjavonjuwie (swisssaeopgaui pyeongyangsaenghwal chillnyeon].* Translated by Sangsun Lim and Wonsun Kwon. Seoul: Huine.

Agency of Statistics of the Republic of Kazakhstan. 2018. *GDP and holding foreign currency Kazakhstan.*

Babson, Bradley O. 2016. "The North Korean Economic System: Challenges and Issues, International Journal of Korean Studies." *International Journal of Korean Studies* 10 (1): 149–175.

Babson, Bradley O. 2009. "Transformation and Modernization of North Korea: Implications for Future Engagement Policy." In project paper produced as part of the project "Improving Regional Security and Denuclearizing the Korean Peninsula: U.S. Policy Interests and Options." National Committee for North Korea.

Bang, Chan Young. 1995. *The Democratic People's Republic of Korea at a crossroad, Park Young-sa*. Seoul: Bak Young Sa. pp. 99, 232–233, 188–242.

Bang, Chan Young. 2017. *Bold and Audacious Challenge for Chairman Kim [Kim Jong Un wiwonjang ui widaehan dojeon]*. Seoul: Yuwolae Press.

Bang, Chan Young. 2018a. "Bold Challenges and Opportunities of Chairman Kim Jong-un." Speech, Seoul: International Conference on North Korean Economy.

Bang, Chan Young. 2018b. "Why North Korea Can't Follow in Vietnam's Footsteps." *The Diplomat*. Retrieved from https://thediplomat.com/2018/07/why-north-korea-cant-follow-in-vietnams-footsteps/.

Bank of Korea. 2018. Foreign Exchange Reserves.

Beech, Hannah. 2019. "Vietnam Summit Hosts Offer North Korea a Model: Cozy Up to the U.S." *New York Times*. Retrieved from https://www.nytimes.com/2019/02/26/world/asia/trump-kim-vietnam-summit-north-korea-relations.html.

Brown, William. 2018. "Special Report: North Korea's Shackled Economy." *The National Committee on North Korea*. Retrieved from https://www.ncnk.org/resources/briefing-papers/all-briefing-papers/special-report-north-koreas-shackled-economy-2018.

Buncombe, Andrew. 2018. "North Korea says there is 'no way' it will give up nuclear weapons without trust." *Independent*. Retrieved from https://www.independent.co.uk/news/world/asia/north-korea-latest-nuclear-weapons-disarm-united-nations-trust-us-sanctions-a8561371.html.

Channel A. 2018. "Historic Trump-Kim summit set for Jun 12 in Singapore". Retrieved from https://www.channelnewsasia.com/news/world/trump-kim-summit-to-take-place-in-singapore-jun-12-10222378.

CNBC. 2018. "China applies its own maximum pressure policy on Pyongyang". Retrieved from https://www.cnbc.com/2018/04/07/china-applies-its-own-maximum-pressure-policy-on-pyongyang.html.

Dekleva, Kenneth B. 2019. "A Hypothetical Letter from Chairman Kim Jong Un to President Donald Trump". *38 North*. Retrieved from https://www.38north.org/2019/06/kdekleva060719/.

Delury, John. 2018. "Kim Jong-un Has a Dream. The U.S. Should Help Him Realize It." *The New York Times*. Retrieved from https://www.nytimes.com/2018/09/21/opinion/kim-jong-un-moon-economic-development-north-korea-denuclearization.html.

Fifield, Anna. 2019. *The Great Successor: The Divinely Perfect Destiny of Brilliant Comrade Kim Jong Un*. New York: Public Affairs. p. 276.

GDP and holding foreign currency Korea in 2018. The Bank of Korea.

Gu, Haewoo. 2013. *Kim Jong Un's regime and North Korea's reform and opening up. [Kimjongun chaejaewa bukhanui gaehyeokgaebang]*. Seoul: Nanam.

Harris, Bryan. 2018. "Sanctions-hit North Korea faces crisis over hard currency." *Financial Times*. Retrieved from https://www.ft.com/content/db90592e-3876-11e8-8eee-e06bde01c544.

Hisasi, Hirai. 2012. *Kim Jong Un regime [Kimjongun chaejae]*. Translated by Gyemun Baek and Yongbin Lee. Seoul: Hanul Academy.

Hung Li. 1977. *China's Political Situation and the Power Struggle in Peking*. Lung Men Press.

Jaewon, Kim. 2019. "Ex-North Korean diplomat says Kim will never give up nuclear arms." *Nikkei Asian Review*. Retrieved from https://asia.nikkei.com/Politics/Trump-Kim-Summit/Ex-North-Korean-diplomat-says-Kim-will-never-give-up-nuclear-arms.

Jeong-ho, Lee & Chan, Minnie. 2018. "Kim Jong-un will use nuclear weapons to push for more from West, ex-South Korean negotiator says." *South China Morning Post*. Retrieved from https://www.scmp.com/news/china/diplomacy-defence/article/2143585/kim-jong-un-will-use-nuclear-weapons-push-more-west-ex.

Jongwha, Lee. 2019. "A Practical Approach to North Korean Denuclearization." *Project Syndicate*. Retrieved from https://www.project-syndicate.org/commentary/north-korea-denuclearization-inter-korean-cooperation-by-lee-jong-wha-2019-05.

Jung hoon, L. 2014. *North Korea's Market Price and Inflation-Related Issues*. Seoul: Hanul. pp. 230–231.

Jung, Sanghun. 1990. *The Process of the North Korean Economy [Bukhangyeongjaeui jeongaegwajung]*. Gyungnam University Institute of Far East Affairs.

Jung, Yeongchul. 2004. *North Korea's reform and opening up (dual strategy and practical socialism) [Bukhanui gaehyeokgaebang (leejungjeonryakgwa sillisahoejuui)]*. Seoul: Book Publishing Sunnin.

Kang, David C. 2018. "Why should North Korea give up its nuclear weapons?" *The New York Times*. Retrieved from https://www.nytimes.com/2018/08/22/opinion/north-korea-nuclear-trump.html.

Kaseda, Yoshinori. 2015. "Economic Engagement with North Korea." In *The North Korea Crisis and regional responses*. Edited by Utpal Vyas and Ching-Chang Chen. Honolulu: East-West Center.

Kim, Byung-Yeon. 2017. *Unveiling The North Korean Economy: Collapse and Transition*. Cambridge: Cambridge University Press.

Kim, Jack. 2019. "North Korea's Kim: I don't want my children to bear burden of nuclear arms—report." *Reuters*. Retrieved from https://www.reuters.com/

article/us-northkorea-usa-kim/north-koreas-kim-i-dont-want-my-children-to-bear-burden-of-nuclear-arms-report-idUSKCN1QC0CZ.

KINU. 2017. *Analysis of 2017 North Korea's New Year's Day Speech and Prospect for its Internal and External Policy.*

Korea University Basic Literature Research Team. 2005. 7.1 *Action and North Korea [chill il jochiwa bukhan].* Seoul: Noppigippi.

Kyodo News. 2019. "Kim not giving up nukes, North Korea military officers likely told." Retrieved from https://english.kyodonews.net/news/2019/06/56ba48cc7005-kim-not-giving-up-nukes-n-korea-military-officers-likely-told.html.

Lankov, Andrey. 2009. *North Korea Workout [Bukhanwokaout].* Seoul: Sidaejeongshin.

Lee, Yeonghwi. 2008. *The globalization of the economy from nuclear weapons [Haekmuggirobuteo gyeongjaeui segyehwa].* Seoul: Book publishing Haenam.

Li, Hung. 1977. *China's Political Situation and the Power Struggle in Peking.* Hong Kong: Lung Men Press. p. 107.

Lockie, Alex. 2018. "North Korea falls into $1.7 billion trade deficit with China—but something mysterious is keeping it afloat." *Business Insider.* Retrieved from https://www.businessinsider.com/north-korea-17-billion-china-trade-deficit-suggests-mysterious-funding-2018-2.

Martin, Bradley K. 2019. "How the US president could earn his Nobel." *Asia Times.* Retrieved from https://www.asiatimes.com/2019/06/article/how-the-us-president-could-earn-his-nobel/.

Nam, Seongouk. 2016. *The Food Crisis and Cooperative Farm Reform in Modern North Korea [Hyeondai bukhanui sikryangnangwa hyeopdongnongjang gaehyeok].* Seoul: Hanul Academy.

Nanto, Dick K. 2010. "North Korea: Economic Leverage and Policy Analysis." *US Congress Papers.*

Noland, Marcus. 2017. "Dollarization in North Korea." *Peterson Institute for International Economics.* Retrieved from https://www.piie.com/blogs/north-korea-witness-transformation/dollarization-north-korea.

North Korean Economic Forum. 2005. *Modern North Korean Economic Theory [Hyeondai bukhangyeongjaeroan].* Seoul: Book Publishing Oreum.

Park, Hugeon. 2015. *Reorganization of the North Korean Economy [Bukhan gyeongjaeui jaegusung].* Seoul: Book Publishing Sunin.

Park, Yong-soo. 2009. "The Political Economy of Economic Reform in North Korea." *Australian Journal of International Affairs* 63 (4): 529–549.

Schortgen, Francis. 2017. "The Political Logic of Economic Backwardness in North Korea." *North Korean Review* 13 (2): 48–65.

Silberstein, Benjamin Katzeff. 2019. "Kim Jong-un's speech at the SPA in April 2019." *North Korean Economy Watch.* Retrieved from https://www.nkeconwatch.com/2019/04/14/kim-jong-uns-speech-at-the-spa-in-april-2019/.

Silva, Christina. 2017. "North Korea's Kim Jong Un Is Starving His People to Pay for Nuclear Weapons". *News Week.* Retrieved from https://www.newsweek.com/north-koreas-kim-jong-un-starving-his-people-pay-nuclear-weapons-573015.

Smith, Nicola. 2018. "North Korea warns it will not give up nuclear weapons until US removes 'threat'." *The Telegraph.* Retrieved from https://www.telegraph.co.uk/news/2018/12/21/north-korea-warns-will-not-give-nuclear-weapons-us-removes-threat/.

Stradiotto, Guo. 2007. "The Nature and Direction of Economic Reform in North Korea." *Political Studies* 55: 754–778.

Stricker, Andrea & Albbright, David. 2019. "How North Korea can be convinced to give up nuclear weapons." *NK News.* Retrieved from https://www.nknews.org/2019/01/how-north-korea-can-be-convinced-to-give-up-nuclear-weapons/.

Tudor, Daniel & Pearson, James. 2017. *Capitalist Republic of Korea [Joseonjavonjuuigonghwaguk].* Translated by Byeonggeun Jeon. Seoul: Via Book Publisher.

Willis, James. 2019. "Readers React: Why Kim Jong Un will never give up North Korea's nukes: Moammar Kadafi." *Los Angeles Times.* Retrieved from https://www.latimes.ckom/opinion/readersreact/la-ol-le-north-korea-kim-jong-un-kadafi-20190301-story.html.

Wit, Joel S. & Sokolsky, Richard. 2019. "Memo to Donald Trump: It's Time to End-Run Your Advisers on North Korea." *38 North.* Retrieved from https://www.38north.org/2019/05/jwitrsokolsky052219/.

Wolf, Charles, Jr & Levin, Norman D. 2008. "Modernizing the North Korean System. Objectives, Method, and Application." *RAND Corporation.*

World Politics Review. 2019. "Why North Korea Denuclearization Is Such a Long Shot." Retrieved from https://www.worldpoliticsreview.com/insights/27952/why-north-korea-denuclearization-is-such-a-long-shot.

Yang, Mun Su. 2014a. "Chapter 10: JO, Seong Ju 'Marketisation and Gender in North Korea [bukhanui sijanghua-wa gender]'." In *Economy and Society in the Kim Jong Un Era [Kim Jong Un shidaeui gyungjaewa sahoe].* Seoul: Hanul Academy.

Yang, Mun Su. 2014b. "Chapter 1: JO, Dong-ho 'Economic Policy in the Kim Jong Un Era [Kim Jong Un sidae ui gyongjaejeongchaek]'." In *Economy and Society in the Kim Jong Un Era [Kim Jong Un shidaeui gyungjaewa sahoe].* Seoul: Hanul.

Yang, Munsu. 2001. *The structure of the North Korean economy (mechanism of economic development and stagnation). [Bukhangyeongjaeui gujo (gyeongjaegaebalgwa chimchaeui mechanism)].* Seoul: Seoul National University Press and Culture Center.

Yang, Munsu. 2010. *Marketization of the North Korean Economy [Bukhangyeongjaeui sijanghwa].* Seoul: Hanul Academy.

Yang, Munsu. 2014c. *The Economy and Society of Kim Jong Un's Era [Kimjongunsidaeui gyeongjaewa sahoe]*. Seoul: Hanul Acedemy.

Yonhap News Agency. 2018. "N. Korea's hard currency reserves expected to dry up by October: lawmaker." Retrieved from https://en.yna.co.kr/view/AEN20180221003000315.

Yonhap News. 2016. "N. Korea ranks No. 1 for military spending relative to GDP: State Department report." Retrieved from en.yna.co.kr/view/AEN20161223000200315.

Yoon, In Ju. 2015. *The Privatization Phenomenon in North Korea [Bukhanui sayuhau hyonsang]*. Seoul: Korean Academic Information.

Yuwen, Deng. 2018. "Why Kim Jong-un's promise of a nuclear-free North Korea should not be trusted." *South China Morning Post*. Retrieved from https://www.scmp.com/comment/insight-opinion/article/2144623/why-kim-jong-uns-promise-nuclear-free-north-korea-should-not.

CHAPTER 5

Conclusion

This book, at its core, sought to answer the question: "What does it really take for North Korea to survive?" Here, "survival" should be interpreted as not merely sustaining the status quo but transforming into an economically prosperous country and a respected member of the international community. The past 25 years of U.S. attempts at denuclearization talks with North Korea have produced tremendous failure because no viable policy, incorporating the various strategic interests of the key stakeholders (China, Russia, Japan, and South Korea), to guarantee the survival of the regime after ending the nuclear weapons program has been put forward. Today, sanctions are pushing Kim Jong Un to the negotiating table because the inefficient, distorted economy has reached a breaking point. He will soon be faced with a decision between armed provocation or the ultimate demise of the regime—unless he chooses to implement radical reform and opening, culminating in the establishment of North Korea as a new, emerging economic power in Northeast Asia.

From a broad prospective, there are essentially two options to be entertained as possible exit strategies for Kim Jong Un that ensure the survival of the regime. The first is the approach that has been in practice throughout recent decades: safeguarding the legitimacy of the regime with the nuclear weapons program. The second is more radical: obtaining alternative sources of security and legitimacy by embracing a package deal in exchange for giving up nuclear weapons.

C. Y. Bang, *Transition beyond Denuclearisation*,
https://doi.org/10.1007/978-981-15-4316-6_5

1 The Possibility of North Korea's Survival with Weapons of Mass Destruction

First, let us look at the possibility of North Korea's survival with nuclear weapons. As this book has explained in great detail, there is little chance that a nuclear-armed North Korea will survive. Throughout history, all socialist countries have either perished or embraced market-oriented system reform. North Korea has managed to survive thus far by espousing the myth that it has achieved the establishment of a "heaven on Earth" for the worker under a great leader who is incapable of error, while also acquiescing the unofficial, bottom-up process of marketization. Through the strengthening of the state's control mechanisms, the regime has coerced internal loyalty through such apparatuses of terror as the rationing system and ideological indoctrination, the blocking of information not permitted by the state, an alliance of minority elites, and public executions. Externally, enemies are contrived through hostile foreign policy in order justify harsher crackdowns on the inside and to impel the loyalty of the people. The reality the regime must now face is that the myths and control mechanisms that once maintained Kim Jong Un's regime are no longer functioning.

The factors that once ensured the regime's survival have eroded, and the situation has rapidly deteriorated. Harsh economic sanctions, mobilized collectively by the five stakeholder nations, have intensified the distortions of the system to erode the foundations of the regime's stability—depleting hard currencies in the possession of Kim Jong Un that are crucial for survival, heightening inflation and dollarization, expanding unofficial marketization from below and crushing the solidarity of the minority elite, who have ardently supported the Kim Jong Un regime. Dire food shortages in 2019 have also put the regime under extreme pressure, with approximately 10.1 million North Koreans suffering after the worst harvest in 10 years.[1] The system no longer bears any resemblance to its socialist roots, and the legitimacy of the regime itself is in grave danger. Previous hostile tactics like brinkmanship are no longer effective as a source of unity or at the negotiating table, though Kim Jong Un continues to employ them. The loss of these tactical functions would inflict a serious blow to the regime's legitimacy, as this hostility has long been used to solidify loyalty and justify the military-first policy. As the distortions of the system are aggravated further, the regime's foundation will continue to crumble.

The highly-publicized defection of three North Korean security officials, reported in *JoongAng Ilbo* in April 2019, suggests that defection by North Koreans is not just a matter of some individuals who have reached border areas for survival, but a sign of the collapse of the core minority elite, which affects the maintenance of the North Korean regime. In addition, the more than 400 unofficial marketplaces have already made it impossible for the regime to completely block unwanted information. South Korean dramas, movies and numerous other sources of knowledge of the outside, which enter through these marketplaces, have become completely unstoppable, even if the North were to proceed with a tougher crackdown. This situation is causing the North Korean myth to steadily erode due to the gap between the prevailing reality and ideology.

Thus, I have come to the conclusion that North Korea will soon face a grave situation, precipitating calamity and likely pushing Kim Jong Un to resort to armed provocation. Kim Jong Un's changed tone in recent years is believed to have emerged as a result of real desperation. Since 2018, Kim Jong Un has continuously emphasized the need for economic development. As stated earlier, in his New Year 2019 address, he strongly expressed the importance of development, and he has repeatedly emphasized since that economic modernization is the right direction for North Korean society rather than the *byongjin* line (North Korea's dual policy of nuclear and economic development).

It is important to emphasize that the increasingly harsh collectively- and independently-imposed sanctions enforced by UNSC member states over recent years are not the fundamental cause of North Korea's current economic predicament. Sanctions have merely exacerbated the distortions of the fatally-dysfunctional system of the DPRK, revealing its various malaises and defects. Because the distortions of the system are so embedded in its very nature, the lifting of sanctions will not be sufficient to ensure the survival of North Korea unless it is accompanied by radical economic reform and prosperity. Now, even if Kim Jong Un decides to abandon nuclear weapons in order to embrace economic development, he is still faced with two disparate paths to modernization: keeping the current regime intact or implementing reform.

2 Accepting Denuclearization to Maintain the Current Socioeconomic System

Broadly, there are two choices Kim Jong Un faces in the decision to denuclearize: either sustain the current regime or implement radical market-oriented reform of the system. Giving up weapons of mass destruction—including intercontinental missiles, chemical weapon systems and the nuclear weapons program—while maintaining the existing North Korean regime is tantamount to continuing the prevailing North Korean extractive totalitarianism, monolithic leadership and minority alliance system in Pyongyang. Kim Jong Un's legitimacy will continued to stem from *Juche* ideology (self-reliance) and the monolithic leadership system that comes down from his grandfather and father, as he has done in the past. In this case, however, it is impossible to guarantee the viability of the North Korean regime. Due to the fundamental defects of the system, even if denuclearization is accompanied by the lifting of international sanctions and the provision of monetary reward, the survival of the regime cannot be assured.

It should be noted that no socialist country that has achieved rapid, market-oriented economic growth has succeeded without genuine regime change. As we have witnessed in the case of China, North Korea must embrace the transformation into a market socialist system in order for rapid economic growth to take place. If North Korea continues with its totalitarian regime, inter-Korean conflicts cannot be resolved, and stability on the Korean Peninsula will be impossible to establish. The purpose of giving up nuclear weapons is to improve the welfare of the people, but because of the critical defects of the current system, North Korea cannot achieve the rapid, sustained economic growth necessary to justify denuclearization.

As stated earlier, in order to achieve spectacular, sustained economic growth, integration with the world economy is essential. If North Korea continues to apply hostile foreign policy, however, integration with the world economy, which is critical to economic modernization, cannot be attained. With the current system maintained, crucial foreign investment will be difficult to entice. To attract foreign capital, favorable foreign investment law must be enacted, based on market-oriented principles. Without transforming hostile foreign policy into amicable, benign relations, Kim Jong Un will surely fail to attract sufficient foreign capital necessary for economic development. It should be noted that North Korea's hostile foreign relations do not stem from its possession of nuclear weapons. On the contrary, the development of the nuclear weapons program is a direct result of the DPRK's hostile foreign policy. Therefore, even if denuclearization takes place, it will not guarantee the establishment of amicable foreign policy, without which investment cannot be attracted.

In short, even if North Korea decides to give up its nuclear weapons program, it can never escape its distorted economic system and integrate with the world economy as long as it maintains its existing system—this is simply not an option for survival. What Kim Jong Un calls a "strong state" and "welfare improvement for the people" through rapid economic development is untenable to pursue in parallel with a military-first policy. Thus, modernization cannot be achieved without a paradigm change in the nature of the regime. So, what are the choices with which Kim Jong Un is now faced?

3 A Survival Strategy Through Rapid Economic Development

The only option for the survival of the North Korean regime is to establish a strategic plan for economic development with the aim of shifting to a market socialist system as a condition for giving up nuclear weapons. Just as Deng Xiao Peng's famed tour of southern China to inspect and strengthen reform and openness enabled China to become what it is today, Kim Jong Un has the chance to write a new history of the DPRK through "economic modernization" and secure a new source of legitimacy for his reign. If Kim Jong Un makes this choice, it will not only ensure his survival but also be recorded in world history as a great achievement on the part of his bold and courageous decision.

In order for North Korea to choose an economic reform line based on the global market order, a blueprint for economic development must be put forth to achieve the transformation of the country's own means of production and liberalization of the labor market. The blueprint should include a strategy to achieve an average annual economic growth rate of at least 10%. This is comparable to that achieved by South Korea and China during peak eras, the fastest growth witnessed in 20 to 30 years, and is sufficient to drastically improve the welfare of the people. If he succeeds in realizing this goal, Kim Jong Un's legitimacy will no longer stem from the monolithic leadership system that he inherited from Kim Il Sung but from his achievements in achieving dynamic economic growth and development. However, such a feat will be impossible without the unyielding participation of the stakeholder nations—Kim Jong Un's survival without nuclear weapons depends upon the security guarantees and development funds they can offer. The cooperation and compensation that North Korea must receive from the stakeholder nations in order to accept a proposal for denuclearization must entail both guarantees of security and development funds necessary to ensure market-oriented economic reform.

Kim Jong Un must be assured that the two Koreas will settle their current relationship of hostility and work toward shared growth based on a new relationship of mutual cooperation and inter-dependence by first entering into a peace treaty. Following this, both the North and the South must carry out radical arms reduction measures, with the resulting financial and human resources saved from current levels being utilized toward modernizing North Korea's economy. U.S. forces stationed in South Korea should be withdrawn from the country once North Korea's denuclearization is complete, and the two Koreas must stipulate the recognition of two different systems with no challenge to respective sovereignty within their constitutions, clearly enunciating the principle that neither of the parties will integrate, nor unite the other against their will. Additionally, China and Russia must reconfirm their treaty obligations as North Korea's allies, while Japan and North Korea must establish normalized diplomatic relations. Furthermore, the U.S. must normalize relations with the DPRK by establishing diplomatic recognition.

In order to provide a sufficient development fund, South Korea must bear the major share of $30 billion a year, for a total of $300 billion over the next ten years. Of the 30 billion dollars to be paid each year, $10 billion is to be paid in cash and the remaining $20 billion in the form of vouchers to be used for infrastructure construction. The $10 billion paid to North Korea should be used to employ and pay wages to workers mobilized in the construction of infrastructure, to administer social security policies, and to develop human resources, while the $20 billion paid in vouchers must be used to pay the expenses of Korean corporations, selected through a bidding process, participating in the construction of North Korea's infrastructure. Japan must also resolve the issue of reparations for colonial rule. When calculating the current value of the $500 million previously paid by Japan to South Korea, in the form of grants and loans, North Korea should receive at least $30 billion as compensation, in the form of grants and loans. The remaining stakeholder nations must support North Korea in the process of securing additional loans as needed from international monetary organizations.

These external prerequisites, or necessary conditions, however, will not succeed in achieving peace, stability and economic prosperity on the Korean Peninsula if North Korea does not first fulfill certain internal prerequisites—sufficient conditions for economic reform and opening. First and foremost, the critical distortions of the dysfunctional economy must be rectified to ensure that integration with the world economy can take place. As described in detail in Chap. 4, the DPRK must enact a Foreign Enterprise Investment Act, based on market principles, specifying provisions for joint ventures, remittances, land leases, corporate bankruptcies and international arbitration to resolve disputes between companies. Then, reform geared towards the creation of a market-oriented system must be implemented in self-contained, isolated special economic zones (SEZs) in order to minimize the shocks of opening to the state. The limited development funds must first be allocated to SEZs, where infrastructure will be developed and privatization—including the establishment of joint ventures, a free labor market and free economic activity—will be introduced along with radical investment law based on market principles.

4 A Blueprint for "Transaction" and "Transformation" Led by the U.S.

The peaceful resolution of the North Korea nuclear crisis—complete, verifiable, and irreversible denuclearization (CVID)—will require that the United States secure the active participation and unyielding commitment of all four of the remaining stakeholder nations (South Korea, China, Russia and Japan) and take the initiative to formulate a blueprint to establish a "bright future" for North Korea. To accomplish this, the stakeholders must first align under a shared understanding of what this "bright future" entails—namely that denuclearization would be accompanied by sustained peace, stability and economic prosperity on the Korean Peninsula. While all members of the Six-party Talks may share this overarching goal, their individual interests and security concerns differ. The U.S. has singularly emphasized the denuclearization of the DPRK through the application of economic and military threat without addressing the "carrots" of survival with economic reform. China, Russia, and South Korea, however, will never support a policy that involves denuclearization at the cost of regime collapse.

Failing to compose a shared policy, the U.S. so far has not effectively utilized the "sticks" and "carrots" of the stakeholders to denuclearize North Korea. In order to persuade Kim Jong Un, the U.S. must recognize and utilize both the collective threats and benefits that can be offered by the stakeholder nations to convince Kim Jong Un that the cost of retaining nuclear weapons would be so detrimental to his survival chances that he should embrace the benefits of denuclearization. Therefore, the U.S. must take the initiative in aligning all of the stakeholders via a shared policy that ensures a credible opportunity for regime survival without nuclear weapons—economic modernization in exchange for dismantlement of the nuclear program.

Thus far, North Korea has attempted only transactional, piecemeal deals to alleviate the pain of sanctions enforcement in its talks with the U.S., and has never been able to present a blueprint that involves reform of the regime. The only way to ensure the survival of the regime is if Kim Jong Un formulates a plan that clearly enunciates the elements of a "bright future" without nuclear weapons and outlines the necessary measures to attain this future. In this way, the regime would avoid the risk of regime collapse after denuclearization and successfully incorporate North Korea into the global market order system, which is a condition that all five stakeholder countries can agree on.

Modernization will require more than a mere transactional agreement; it will demand genuine transformation of North Korea into a market socialist system, radically altering the ruling ideology of *Juche* (self-reliance) and the *byongjin* line, allowing for the introduction of legislation based on free-market principles and for investment in sustainable development of business and infrastructure. Such radical political and economic reform, accompanied by the relinquishment of all weapons of mass destruction and routine inspections by the International Atomic Energy Agency (IAEA), would be compensated by the stakeholders' joint, comprehensive economic and security package. In order for North Korea to pave a foundation for sustainable economic growth, carry out complete dismantlement of the nuclear weapons program, and to account for the significant length of time required for IAEA's nuclear dismantlement and inspection process, a minimum duration of 10 years must be stipulated.

Ultimately, Kim Jong Un's survival is contingent upon his ability to enter into negotiations with the stakeholders, led by the U.S., to guarantee a chance at economic prosperity and peace without the nuclear weapons program. The implementation of the blueprint for North Korea's economic modernization, involving successful integration with the world economy, reforming the inefficient system, would be tantamount to a "bright future" for both North Korea and the five parties involved, as well as a path to permanent peace on the Korean Peninsula. Kim Jong Un's bold and audacious decision to give up nuclear weapons for economic modernization will provide him with a new source of legitimacy. I trust that, *if he were to accept this blueprint*, he would make the rational choice to embrace denuclearization in exchange for spectacular economic growth and seize the opportunity to be reassessed as one of the most successful leaders in world history.

Note

1. World Food Program, *Democratic People's Republic of Korea (DPRK)—FAO/WFP Joint Rapid Food Security Assessment*, 3 May 2019.

Index[1]

A

Acquiescence, 13, 23, 39, 41, 53, 75
Agricultural sector, 40, 52, 53, 60n43, 138–139
Agriculture, 38, 40, 51, 60n43, 69, 129
Aid, 16, 37, 82, 87, 113
Airport, 124, 125, 131, 132, 134
Alliance, 89, 104, 150, 152
Analysis, 5, 8, 9, 17–37, 48, 54, 67, 88, 90, 107–112
Arbitration, 120, 128, 131, 155
Arduous March, 3, 9, 36, 40–42, 67, 69, 76, 83, 103
Armed conflict, 2, 81
Armed provocation, 91, 111, 149
Army, 35, 38, 79
Authoritarian, 79, 87
Authoritarianism, 120, 121
Authority, 18–20, 24, 25, 29, 31, 72, 80, 114, 115, 129, 131, 135, 139
Autonomy, 42, 118
Average minimum GDP growth rate, 105, 122, 123

B

Bank, 24, 31, 38, 46, 48, 82, 134, 136
Bankrupt/bankruptcy, 115, 120, 128, 131, 155
Benefit, 5, 10, 88, 89, 91, 108–111, 120, 126, 128, 131, 140, 156
Benign oversight, 13, 23, 36, 39, 41, 53, 75–78
Blueprint, 3, 4, 7, 8, 11, 88, 105, 121, 125, 126, 129, 139, 141, 153, 155–157
Border, 51, 73, 123, 128, 151
Bottom-up marketization, 9, 16, 36, 77–78
Boycott, 81, 109
Brainwash, 70
Bright future, 6, 68, 88, 91, 103, 106–108, 111, 155–157
Brinkmanship, 90, 124, 150
Bureaucracy, 113, 131
Bureaucratic, 16, 23, 25, 26, 42, 49, 51, 70, 72, 73, 124, 127, 128, 131, 133, 136

[1] Note: Page numbers followed by 'n' refer to notes.

C. Y. Bang, *Transition beyond Denuclearisation*,
https://doi.org/10.1007/978-981-15-4316-6

Bureaucratic control mechanisms, 25, 70, 72
Business, 7, 13, 41, 55n6, 78, 81, 112, 115, 136, 137, 156
Byongjin, 71, 107, 151, 156

C

Calamity, 16, 54, 68, 126, 151
Calculation, 9, 10, 19–21, 87–88, 90, 91, 110, 112, 135
Capitalism, 9, 21, 22, 28–30, 33, 55n5, 75
Carrot, 5, 68, 87–90, 106, 108–111, 139, 140, 155, 156
Cash, 46, 48, 104, 154
Censure, 81, 109
Central planning, 18–20, 22–25, 51
Chairman, 8, 10, 45, 52, 70, 88, 108, 114, 127, 129, 139, 141
Challenge, 17, 18, 25, 31, 114–116, 121, 129
Chemical weapons, 110, 152
China, 3, 6, 8, 17, 21, 22, 30, 31, 34, 35, 39, 40, 44, 47, 49, 50, 52, 58n29, 69, 72, 82–85, 87, 89, 90, 104, 105, 108, 109, 113, 114, 117–121, 125, 130, 134, 137, 139, 140, 149, 152–155
Circulation, 46, 48, 74
Civil engineering, 133
Coalition, 9, 36–38, 68, 78–80, 90
Collapse, 8–10, 31, 34, 35, 39–48, 51, 54, 60n43, 67–91, 106, 108, 111, 117, 151, 156
Collapse of the Soviet Union, 16, 29, 39–48
Commodities, 16, 44, 83, 135
Communications, 24, 38, 128, 131, 132
Communism, 24, 31, 32, 39, 43, 55n5, 75
Communist Party, 2, 22, 24–26, 29, 90, 114, 118, 130
Community, 3, 40, 49, 69, 75, 81, 83, 90, 111, 116, 120, 149
Compensation, 6, 18, 19, 106, 110, 154
Complete, Verifiable, Irreversible Denuclearization (CVID), 124, 139, 155
Compliance, 87
Conditions, 4, 5, 7, 17, 18, 23, 26, 40, 41, 51–53, 57n16, 67–69, 74, 84, 103–105, 107–113, 125, 130, 132, 153, 155, 156
Conflict, 2, 11, 75, 81, 126, 152
Construction, 23, 31, 80, 107, 124–126, 130, 132–134, 136, 154
Consumer goods, 43, 135
Contradiction, 7, 35, 42, 47, 52, 68, 70–71, 118
Control, 15, 16, 19, 21, 25, 26, 30, 32, 34–37, 41, 42, 48, 49, 51, 52, 55n6, 60n43, 67, 68, 70, 72–75, 77, 79, 82, 84, 90, 115, 119, 123, 124, 127, 131–134, 136, 150
Corporation, 24, 38, 45, 48, 118, 119, 127–129, 132, 136, 154
Cost, 5, 10, 20, 42, 61n43, 71, 81, 83, 88, 91, 108–111, 117, 125, 126, 129, 133, 135, 140, 156
Cost and benefit, 10
Crisis, 17, 26, 27, 30, 31, 39, 40, 50, 52, 54n4, 68, 70, 83, 84, 87, 106, 111, 155
Currency, 19, 30, 31, 39, 41, 43, 45–48, 50, 52, 62n59, 78, 83, 119, 120, 128, 131, 134–136, 142n17, 150

D

Defect, 20, 114, 151, 152
Defector, 36, 51, 70, 73, 77, 85, 93n24
Defense, 35, 61n43, 71, 72
Deficit, 44, 45, 49, 50, 52, 69, 78, 83, 134
Demand, 19, 20, 23, 31, 36, 40, 58n29, 77, 90, 91, 118, 129–132, 135, 138, 140, 156
Demise, 13, 14, 21, 27, 34, 40, 43, 103, 105, 149
Democratic People's Republic of Korea (DPRK), 1–6, 9–11, 13–54, 67, 68, 70, 72, 75, 80, 81, 83, 85, 87–91, 92n17, 103–107, 109–111, 113–117, 122, 126–129, 132, 133, 138–141, 151, 153–155, 157n1
Deng Xiaoping, 113, 117, 118, 120, 130
Denuclearization, 1, 4, 5, 7, 8, 10, 67, 68, 80, 81, 83, 87–89, 91, 103–141, 149, 152–157
Denuclearize, 1, 9, 10, 114, 116, 152, 156
Destabilizing effects, 3, 117, 119, 121, 123
Deterrence, 71, 72, 75, 85, 89, 104
Development, 1, 3–6, 8, 9, 13, 22, 23, 30, 32, 35, 55n5, 58–59n29, 60–61n43, 68, 71–72, 75, 80, 81, 88, 90, 104–107, 109, 110, 113, 114, 116–119, 121–141, 151–156
Development fund, 3, 6, 7, 90, 91, 104, 105, 109, 110, 113, 117, 119, 121–126, 133, 135, 136, 140, 154, 155
Dictator, 71
Dictatorship, 24, 39, 75, 118
Diplomacy, 88
Diplomatic relations, 89, 109, 154
Disarm, 87
Disarmament, 110, 140
Disintegration, 9, 16, 17, 45, 53, 67–91, 123, 124
Dismantlement, 7, 103, 105, 106, 109, 111, 125, 139, 156
Disparity, 45–49, 51, 54, 83, 114, 123, 126
Distortion, 7, 9, 14, 16, 17, 19, 23, 33, 37–53, 67, 79, 113, 115, 121, 150, 151, 155
Dollarization, 46, 47, 49, 67, 83, 90, 136, 150
Dollars, 43, 46–48, 83, 133, 135, 137, 154
Domestic legitimacy, 10, 35, 72, 79, 89
Donju, 36, 38, 41, 47, 49–53, 62n59, 136
Dysfunction, 7

E

Economic development, 1, 3, 4, 6–9, 22, 23, 30, 59n29, 68, 72, 75, 88, 104, 106, 107, 109, 110, 113, 114, 116, 119, 121, 122, 124–127, 133–137, 140, 151–155
Economic reform, 2, 6–8, 13, 18, 22, 29, 31, 34, 42, 54, 75, 111, 113, 118, 120–121, 123, 125, 128, 130, 137, 140, 151, 153–156
Economy, 3, 13, 16–37, 39–48, 51–53, 67, 103, 112–121, 127–139, 149
Education, 2, 15, 25, 35, 55n6, 73, 125, 136, 137
Electricity, 43, 84, 124, 131

Elite, 3, 17, 36, 49, 70, 78–80, 90, 150, 151
Employment, 15, 123, 128, 135, 136, 141
Energy, 40, 41, 49, 50, 62n59, 81
Enterprise, 13, 18–20, 30, 41, 42, 53, 61n46, 115, 120, 123, 124, 131, 136, 137
Entrepreneur, 125, 131
Erosion, 8, 10, 34–36, 42, 67–80, 103
Execute, 108, 109, 115, 137
Execution, 2, 25, 31, 49, 70, 72, 129, 150
Expert, 10, 48, 67, 70, 82, 88, 105, 113, 125, 129, 137, 138, 141
Expert committee, 105, 129, 141
Exploitation, 16, 24, 38, 49, 51, 69, 84
Export, 40, 44, 49, 50, 52, 69, 81–83, 119, 131, 134, 135
Extraction system, 75
Extractive, 9, 23, 27, 37–38, 60n43, 79, 80, 84, 90, 152

F

Facility/facilities, 84, 126, 127, 132, 134, 141
Factory/factories, 38, 40, 41, 60n43, 84
Failure, 13–54, 121, 128, 149
Famine, 3, 26, 27, 40, 42, 51, 54n4, 69
Fifield, Anna, 88
Fiscal policy, 134–136
Fish, 41, 133
Fluctuation, 135
Food, 21, 25, 32, 39, 40, 44, 45, 49, 51–53, 54n4, 60n43, 67, 69, 74, 77, 80, 82, 84, 136, 138, 139, 150
Food supplies, 49, 138, 139
Forces, 8, 29, 32, 38, 109, 117, 124, 133, 137, 138, 154
Foreign capital, 113, 119, 120, 125, 131, 152
Foreign currency, 45, 46, 48, 50, 78, 83, 119, 120, 128, 131, 134–136, 142n17
Foreign currency reserve, 50, 78, 134–136
Foreign expert, 129, 138
Foreign investment, 115, 119, 120, 131, 152
Foreign policy, 5, 74, 75, 106, 113, 120, 124, 141, 150, 152, 153
Foundation, 8, 10, 35, 38, 72, 91, 105, 114, 122, 124, 150, 156
Framework, 8, 22–27, 37, 89, 104, 105, 109, 111, 139
Freedom, 21, 25, 128
Free labor market, 121, 127, 128, 131, 155
Fund, 3, 6, 7, 9–11, 36, 44, 50, 51, 60n43, 69, 75, 78, 80, 83, 84, 88, 90, 91, 104–106, 109, 110, 113, 117, 119, 121–126, 130, 133–136, 140, 141, 154, 155

G

Gap, 47, 50, 51, 58–59n29, 69, 84, 114, 117, 123, 126, 141, 151
GDP growth rate, 105, 122, 123, 141
Gender, 52, 77–78
Goods, 16, 18–20, 23, 25, 38, 40–46, 48–50, 56n6, 60n43, 80, 83, 84, 132, 134–136
Gorbachev, Mikhail, 3, 42, 61n46, 74, 75, 117
Government expenditure, 45, 50, 134
Grain, 44, 51, 53, 74, 77, 84, 139
Gross domestic product (GDP), 6, 15, 17, 23, 44, 48, 50, 52, 57n14,

67, 69, 71, 78, 83, 90, 105, 114, 116, 117, 122–124, 129, 133, 141, 142n17
Growth, 3, 5–7, 15, 17, 18, 30, 38, 45, 52, 58–59n29, 60–61n43, 83–85, 90, 103, 105, 106, 109, 110, 113, 114, 116, 119, 120, 122–124, 126, 129, 132, 133, 138, 141, 152–154, 156, 157
Growth rate per annum, 110, 122, 123

H
Hanoi, 88, 114
Health, 45, 55n6, 61n43
Heaven on Earth, 70, 88, 120, 150
Heavy industry, 24, 38, 60n43
Hierarchy, 77–78
Higher education, 137
Hostility, 75, 116, 150, 154
Human resources, 23, 58–59n29, 129, 137–138, 141, 154
Human rights, 15, 36, 49, 51, 72–74, 81, 82, 84, 90, 109, 116
Hyperinflation, 43, 45–47, 49, 67, 83

I
Ideology, 3, 5–7, 9, 10, 16, 22, 24–26, 32, 34–35, 37, 39, 48, 68, 70–71, 75, 90, 103, 114–116, 120, 122, 124, 151, 152, 156
Import, 16, 43, 44, 49, 50, 52, 53, 74, 82–84, 135, 136
Improvement, 7, 9, 13, 14, 23, 31–34, 42–43, 120, 122, 132, 153
Improvement measures, 13, 23, 33
Income, 15, 24, 30, 38, 40, 43, 45–51, 73, 80, 83, 84, 114, 123–126, 133, 135, 136, 138
Income gap, 47, 114, 123, 126
Industry, 23, 24, 31, 38, 50, 55n6, 60n43, 76, 80, 116, 131, 133, 134, 136, 138
Inflation, 43, 45–47, 50, 90, 134, 135, 150
Influx, 113, 115, 119
Information, 10, 18–20, 24, 35, 49, 51, 68, 70, 73, 74, 85, 116–118, 123, 136, 150, 151
Information technology, 137
Infrastructure, 31, 59n29, 62n59, 90, 119, 122, 124–126, 129–136, 141, 154–156
Inherit, 115
Inheritance, 42
Inminban, 35, 36, 73
Inspection, 81, 109, 139, 156
Integration, 104, 112–121, 126–139, 141, 152, 155, 157
Integration with the world economy, 112–121, 127–139, 141, 152, 155, 157
International Atomic Energy Agency (IAEA), 139, 156
Investment, 20, 41, 50, 58–59n29, 62n59, 75, 115, 119, 120, 122, 125, 126, 128, 130–133, 138, 152, 153, 155, 156
Isolation, 81, 104, 109

J
Jangmadang, 32, 45, 48, 49, 74, 76, 77, 83
Japan, 8, 55n5, 82, 87, 90, 104, 109, 117, 125, 139, 149, 154, 155
Job security, 123, 133

Joint venture, 119, 127, 128, 131, 138, 155
Juche, 3–6, 9, 16, 31, 32, 37–39, 68, 70–71, 75, 80, 90, 103, 115, 116, 120–122, 152, 156
Justification, 10, 87, 122, 124, 125

K
Kazakhstan, 1, 17, 21, 114, 129, 135, 137, 142n17
Kim Il Sung, 3, 9, 15, 17, 19, 20, 32, 38–40, 60–61n43, 71, 103, 104, 115, 120, 153
Kim Jong Il, 3, 9, 17, 32, 33, 45, 71, 80, 87, 103
Kim Jong Un, 1, 13, 67, 103, 149
Korean economy, 13, 14, 16, 17, 22, 23, 33, 34, 37, 38, 41–43, 46, 49, 51–53, 57n14, 62n59, 67, 83, 84, 91, 103, 110, 113, 123
Korean Peninsula, 5, 8, 33, 87, 89, 110, 139, 140, 152, 155, 157
Korean War, 2, 37
Kornai, János, 6, 9, 22–29, 72

L
Laborer, 45–48, 124, 128, 133, 138, 141
Labor force, 38, 117, 124, 133, 138
Law of value, 19–20, 56n7
Leadership, 7, 10, 16, 19, 32, 34, 36, 38, 39, 50, 52, 68, 75, 77–80, 90, 103, 105, 108, 118, 120, 130, 152, 153
Leading industries, 133
Lease, 23, 120, 131, 155
Legacy, 14, 80, 89, 107, 118
Legislation, 82, 120, 128, 131, 156
Legitimacy, 3, 9, 10, 15, 34, 35, 48, 54, 67, 68, 71, 72, 79, 89, 90, 104, 107, 110, 114–116, 120–122, 141, 149, 150, 152, 153, 157
Lesson, 113–121, 141
Liquidation, 120, 128, 131
Loan, 17, 41, 104, 125, 136, 154, 155
Logistics, 132, 134
Loyalty, 25, 38, 77, 78, 90, 119, 150

M
Macroeconomic, 16, 43, 51, 52, 136
Management, 33, 34, 42, 52, 78, 119, 127, 128, 138
Manufacturing, 16, 43–45, 50, 52, 74, 84
Market economy, 14, 20, 24, 31, 41, 51, 112, 119, 120, 123, 127–131, 134, 137
Marketization, 9, 16, 23, 24, 28, 36, 39–48, 53, 54n4, 57n14, 57n16, 68, 75–78, 103, 150
Market-oriented reform, 3, 11, 13, 14, 22, 27, 29, 30, 33, 43, 53, 105, 113–116, 118, 119, 121–140, 150, 152, 154
Market socialism, 5–7, 10, 21, 22, 27, 29–33, 58n29, 91, 112–122
Market socialist, 21, 22, 24, 30, 36, 105, 106, 110, 113, 121, 122, 152, 153, 156
Means of production, 18–24, 26–30, 32, 37–39, 41, 53, 60n43, 62n59, 153
Mechanism, 23, 25, 26, 49, 67, 68, 70, 72–75, 77, 90, 123, 150
Mediation, 128
Merchant, 32, 45–48, 78
Micro economic, 15
Military, 5, 9, 14, 15, 35, 36, 38, 50, 61n43, 71, 72, 75, 76, 80, 81, 85, 87, 89, 90, 104, 109, 115,

116, 118, 124, 126, 129–130, 132, 133, 136, 139, 141, 155
Military exercise, 81, 89, 104, 109
Military-first policy, 36, 76, 80, 124, 150, 153
Military-industrial complex, 60n43, 61n43
Military officials, 129–130
Minister, 115
Minority, 150–152
Missile, 16, 49, 81, 82, 85, 110, 152
Modernization, 1, 3, 5–7, 10, 11, 13, 54, 57n16, 71, 87, 88, 91, 103–141, 151–153, 156, 157
Modernize, 4, 76, 116, 119, 126, 129, 132, 137, 139
Monetary policy, 31, 41, 134–136
Money, 31, 47, 48, 56n6, 82
Monolithic, 70, 77, 120, 152, 153
Moon Jae-in, 82
Mosquito net, 128
Myth, 150, 151

N
Nationalization, 22, 24, 25, 39
Nationalize, 26
Natural resources, 38, 137
Nature, 9, 13, 14, 16, 18, 21–23, 26, 29, 32, 37–38, 40, 75, 79, 81, 84, 85, 87–91, 106, 121, 140, 151, 153
Nazarbayev, Nursultan, 1
Necessary condition, 7, 57n16, 104, 107–112, 155
Negotiation, 3, 11, 68, 72, 80, 85, 124, 125, 156
Normalized relations, 106
North Korea, 2, 14, 67, 103, 149
Nouveau rich, 38, 47, 78
Nuclear, 8, 35, 71–73, 80–82, 85, 87, 90, 104, 106, 107, 110, 111, 122, 125, 139, 140, 151, 155, 156
Nuclear weapons, 4–7, 9, 11, 54, 67, 68, 71–72, 80, 81, 85, 88, 89, 91, 103–111, 114, 117, 135, 139–141, 149–154, 156, 157
Nuclear weapons program, 1, 4, 5, 8, 10, 13, 17, 54, 68, 71–72, 81, 85, 87–91, 103–108, 110, 111, 114, 141, 149, 152, 153, 156, 157

O
Oil, 40, 44, 50, 83
Opening, 3, 4, 6, 9–11, 13, 14, 31, 34, 43, 53, 54, 57n16, 88, 103, 105, 106, 110, 111, 113–141, 149, 155
Output, 17, 20, 45, 50–53, 69, 132
Oversight, 13, 36, 41, 53, 75–78
Ownership, 18–20, 24, 27–30, 36–38, 41, 42, 55–56n6, 118, 131

P
Party, 2, 7, 22, 24, 25, 29, 30, 32, 36, 37, 41, 71, 77, 78, 90, 104, 107, 118–121, 129–130
Party officials, 48, 72
Peace treaty, 104, 109, 116, 140, 154
Personnel, 90, 125, 128, 132, 136, 141
Piecemeal, 140, 156
Police, 36, 73, 85
Policy, 1, 3, 5, 6, 8, 29–31, 33, 36, 41–43, 46, 52, 54n4, 68, 71, 72, 74–76, 80, 88–90, 104–109, 111, 113, 114, 119, 120, 124, 129, 134–136, 140, 141, 149–153, 156

Political reform, 6, 7, 117–118, 127, 130
Politics, 5, 8, 27, 32
Populace, 70, 80, 123
Population, 15, 36, 37, 39–41, 49, 53, 60n43, 70, 74–76, 79, 80, 85, 90, 126, 137, 138
Port, 126, 132
Power, 9, 13, 16, 19, 24–26, 35–38, 45, 49, 71, 72, 78–80, 85, 87–90, 105, 115, 119, 122, 125, 126, 138, 149
Power plant, 125, 126
Precondition, 6, 7, 10, 11, 75, 112–121
Prerequisite, 19, 115, 122, 130, 132, 155
Pressure, 4, 5, 7, 10, 14, 40, 49, 80, 81, 83, 85, 87, 89, 90, 104, 108, 109, 130, 139, 150
Private sector, 30, 39, 45, 47, 51, 62n59, 123, 127
Privatization, 13, 39, 41, 55n6, 115, 119, 121, 123, 127–129, 136, 155
Productivity, 31, 42, 53, 138, 139
Promise, 58n29, 70, 80, 87, 88, 108–110
Propaganda, 15, 35, 38
Property, 55–56n6, 60n43, 73
Property rights, 28, 55n6, 128
Provision, 3, 6, 38, 104, 105, 109, 120–123, 127, 128, 131, 138, 152, 155
Provocation, 85, 91, 111, 149, 151
Public administration, 137
Punishment, 25, 49, 68, 72, 81, 123
Punitive, 81, 107, 109
Putin, Vladimir, 80
Pyongyang, 14, 35, 38, 79–82, 92n17, 107, 114, 126, 152

R

Railway, 124, 125
Ration, 51, 69
Rational, 9–11, 18–21, 91, 107, 108, 110, 157
Rationality, 87–90, 107–108
Rationing system, 25, 49, 51, 69, 70, 72, 74, 90, 123, 124, 150
Raw materials, 20, 43, 136
Real estate, 133
Reform, 2–4, 6–11, 13–54, 75, 88, 103, 105, 106, 110–141, 149–151, 153–156
Reform of the system, 8, 23, 26, 29, 42, 53, 75, 115, 116, 120, 152
Reform within the system, 14, 39, 42, 117
Regime, 1, 3–5, 7–11, 13, 15, 16, 22, 24, 26, 32–37, 39, 42–44, 46, 49–51, 53, 54, 60n43, 67–76, 78–81, 83–91, 103–111, 113, 115–118, 120, 121, 124, 128, 130, 133, 139, 140, 149–153, 156
Relocation, 128
Remittance, 50, 73, 82, 120, 128, 131, 155
Reparation, 90, 109, 154
Republic, 2, 118
Reserves, 50, 69, 78, 83, 113, 134–136
Resources, 10, 18, 19, 23, 30, 32, 38, 41, 58–59n29, 78, 79, 84, 85, 90, 106, 126, 129, 133, 134, 137–138, 141, 154
Revenue, 36, 45, 49–51, 69, 81, 84, 125, 134, 136
Reward, 5, 87, 89, 152
Rice, 43, 46, 47, 50, 51, 53, 69, 82, 135
Rivalry, 14–15, 116

Roads, 103, 106, 107, 111, 123–125, 131, 132, 134
Russia, 8, 35, 39, 72, 82, 85, 87, 89, 104, 105, 108, 109, 117, 125, 134, 139, 149, 154, 155

S
Sanctions, 5, 7, 9, 10, 14, 16–17, 37, 44, 49–54, 67–70, 72, 78, 80–85, 87, 89–91, 104, 105, 109, 111–113, 139, 149–152, 156
Scenario, 9, 40, 67–91, 106–112
Security, 2, 9, 41, 51, 54n4, 73, 77, 87, 88, 91, 104, 105, 108, 123, 124, 129, 133, 149, 151, 154–156
Security guarantees, 6, 89, 91, 104, 106, 107, 109, 113, 154
Shared policy, 68, 106–109, 111, 140, 156
Shocks, 40–42, 52, 70, 119, 127, 155
Shortage, 40, 41, 43, 44, 49–51, 53, 60n43, 67, 69, 74, 77, 82, 84, 150
Singapore, 3, 108
Six-party Talks, 8, 85, 107, 108, 139, 155
Small coalition, 9, 36–38, 49, 68, 78–80, 90
Socialism, 3, 5–7, 9, 10, 15, 17, 21–33, 37–39, 41, 55n5, 58n29, 60n43, 79, 87, 91, 103, 112–122
Socialist, 2, 3, 5, 7, 9, 13, 14, 16–42, 44, 45, 48, 49, 53, 57n14, 60n43, 74, 75, 79, 103–106, 113, 115, 117–119, 121–123, 130, 134, 140, 141, 150, 152, 153, 156
Socialist party, 2, 119–121
Social security, 124, 125, 136, 154
Socioeconomic, 9, 10, 15, 33, 35, 40, 43–45, 51, 67, 68, 71, 80, 108, 112, 152–153
Soldier, 116
Source of legitimacy, 3, 71, 72, 104, 107, 110, 122, 153, 157
South Korea, 6, 14, 15, 35, 69, 71, 72, 75–77, 81, 82, 85, 87, 89, 90, 104, 105, 108, 109, 114, 116, 117, 123–126, 132, 135, 138–140, 149, 153–155
Soviet Union, 2, 3, 9, 16, 17, 21, 24, 27, 29, 34, 39–48, 53, 60n43, 61n46, 75, 103
Special economic zones (SEZs), 6, 119, 129–131, 141, 155
Speech, 32, 33, 71, 107
Stakeholders, 4, 5, 7, 8, 11, 68, 75, 81, 85, 87–91, 104–111, 121, 122, 125, 139–141, 149, 150, 154–156
State, 1, 2, 4, 7, 8, 13–48, 50–53, 54n4, 55n5, 56n6, 58n29, 60–61n43, 62n59, 67, 69, 71, 72, 74, 77–80, 83–85, 87, 89, 90, 103, 106, 107, 110–115, 118, 119, 123, 124, 126, 127, 129, 132, 136–139, 141, 150, 151, 155
State-owned, 13, 31, 32, 39, 41, 53, 55n6, 127, 129
State sector, 45, 47–48, 127
Stick, 5, 81–82, 87, 106, 108, 110, 111, 139, 140, 156
Sticks and carrots, 89, 139
Strategy/strategies, 8, 83, 87, 90, 91, 121–140, 153–155
Succession, 9, 37, 39, 45, 116
Successor, 115
Sufficient condition, 104–105, 155
Summit, 88, 107, 108

Supply, 19, 20, 23, 31, 36, 43, 49, 50, 58–59n29, 69, 122, 131, 134, 135, 138, 139
Supreme Leader, 3, 14, 60n43, 68, 87, 90, 115
Supreme ruler, 114, 115
Survival, 1, 3–5, 7–11, 15, 27, 33–37, 52, 53, 54n4, 67–91, 104–108, 110, 111, 116, 122, 139, 140, 149–156
Suryong, 37–39
System reform, 112–113, 120, 124, 129, 130, 132, 138, 150

T
Talks, 149, 156
Tax, 41, 128, 134, 139
Technology, 43, 44, 74, 81, 84, 115, 119, 128, 136–138
Telecommunication, 125, 131
Textiles, 49, 81, 83, 133
Threat, 1, 5, 35, 49, 70, 71, 80, 81, 85, 87, 89, 90, 104–106, 108–110, 155, 156
Threats and promises, 108–110
Totalitarian, 19, 23, 27, 28, 37, 79, 152
Totalitarianism, 9, 21, 23, 25–26, 37, 39, 75, 120, 121, 152
Tourism, 23, 134
Trade, 11, 16, 24, 40–44, 50, 52, 54, 56n7, 60n43, 62n59, 69, 75, 78, 80, 82–84, 87, 106, 113, 131, 134, 136, 141
Trade-off, 88, 140
Training, 125, 128, 131, 137, 138
Transaction, 41, 42, 46, 48, 76, 106, 155
Transform, 6, 23, 33, 87, 89, 120–122
Transformation, 6, 7, 14, 17, 22, 23, 27, 28, 34, 87, 104–106, 112–122, 140, 152, 153, 155–157
Transition, 2, 9, 22, 24, 28, 36, 61n46, 91, 117, 123, 124, 136
Transportation, 24, 38, 134
Travel, 128, 131
Trump, Donald, 6, 35, 72, 80, 88, 105, 108

U
Unauthorized information, 49, 68, 74, 123
Unauthorized market, 16, 23, 74
Unification, 126
United Nations Security Council, 81
United Nations (UN), 51, 53, 69
United States (U.S.), 5, 43, 46–48, 55n5, 68, 71, 72, 75, 80–83, 85, 87–89, 104–109, 111, 125, 139, 140, 149, 154–157
University, 2, 41, 137
Unofficial marketization, 28, 103, 150

V
Vietnam, 6, 17, 21, 22, 30, 34, 113–117
Violation, 15, 36, 49, 51, 72–74, 81, 82, 84, 90, 109
Voucher, 104, 154

W
Wage, 20, 46, 47, 125, 128, 133, 135, 136, 154
War, 2, 48, 75, 79, 90
Wealth, 18, 46, 77, 78, 112, 123

Weapons of mass destruction, 85, 107, 110, 135, 139, 140, 150–152, 156
Weapons program, 1, 4, 5, 8, 10, 13, 17, 54, 68, 71–72, 81, 82, 85, 87–91, 103–108, 110, 111, 114, 141, 149, 152, 153, 156, 157
Withdraw, 14, 89, 128, 131, 154
Won, 43, 46, 47, 50, 80–87, 135, 136
Workforce, 133
World economy, 43, 104–106, 112–121, 127–139, 141, 152, 153, 155, 157
World Food Program (WFP), 84

X
Xi Jinping, 80

Y
Yeltsin, Boris, 3

The manufacturer's authorised representative in the EU is Springer Nature Customer Service Centre GmbH, Europaplatz 3, 69115 Heidelberg, Germany. If you have any concerns regarding our products, please contact ProductSafety@springernature.com

Printed and bound by CPI Group (UK) Ltd, Croydon, CR0 4YY
25/09/2026
02222903-0005